D1298124

Language Arts

Grade 2

Printed in the U.S.A.

ISBN 978-0-544-26785-5

12 13 14 2266 22 21 20

4500809595   B C D E F G

Core Skills Language Arts
GRADE 2
Table of Contents

Unit 4: Vocabulary and Usage

Unit 5: Writing

Unit 6: Research Skills

Introduction

Core Skills Language Arts was developed to help your child improve the language skills he or she needs to succeed. The book emphasizes skills in the key areas of

- grammar
- punctuation
- vocabulary
- writing
- research

About the Book

The book is divided into six units:

- Parts of Speech
- Sentences
- Mechanics
- Vocabulary and Usage
- Writing
- Research Skills

Your child can work through each unit of the book, or you can pinpoint areas for extra practice.

Lessons have specific instructions and examples and are designed for your child to complete independently. Grammar lessons range from using nouns and verbs to constructing better sentences. Writing exercises range from the how-to paragraph to the opinion paragraph. With this practice, your child will gain extra confidence as he or she works on daily school lessons or standardized tests.

A thorough answer key is also provided to check the quality of answers.

A Step Toward Success

Practice may not always make perfect, but it is certainly a step in the right direction. The activities in *Core Skills Language Arts* are an excellent way to ensure greater success for your child.

Unit 1: Parts of Speech
Nouns

> A **noun** is a word that names a person, place, or thing.
>
> The words <u>a</u>, <u>an</u>, and <u>the</u> often come before a noun.
>
> *Examples:* a <u>man</u>, an <u>elephant</u>, the <u>yard</u>

Find the nouns, or naming words, below. Write the nouns on the lines.

apple	car	eat	hear	rug	bird	chair
girl	hot	tree	boy	desk	gone	over
truck	came	dirty	grass	pen	up	tiny

1. _____   5. _____   9. _____

2. _____   6. _____   10. _____

3. _____   7. _____   11. _____

4. _____   8. _____   12. _____

Circle the two nouns in each sentence.

13. The girl eats an apple.

14. A bird flies to the tree.

15. A chair is by the desk.

16. A boy sits in the chair.

17. The girl plays with a truck.

Name _____ Date _____

Nouns, part 2

A word that names a person or an animal is called a noun. A word that names a place or a thing is called a noun.

Example: The <u>girl</u> and her <u>dog</u> sat on a <u>bench</u> in the <u>park</u>.

Circle the noun or nouns in each sentence. You should find eleven nouns in all.

1. My sister plays in the park.

2. She rides in a car with our mother.

3. Sometimes our dog goes, too.

4. A boy feeds birds under the trees.

5. Let's go to the playground!

6. I see a cat under the slide.

Look at the nouns you circled. Decide if each noun names a person, a place, a thing, or an animal. Write the noun in the correct space in the chart below.

Person	Place	Thing	Animal

Proper Nouns

A noun is a word that names a person, place, or thing. A **proper noun** is a word that names a special person, place, or thing. A proper noun begins with a capital letter.

Examples:

Noun	**Proper Noun**
girl	Kayla Stone
park	Yellowstone Park
store	Tasty Bread

Find the proper nouns in the box. Write the proper nouns on the lines.

baseball	Bob's Bikes	Bridge Road	children
China	Elf Corn	Gabriel	Lindsey
man	New York City	Oregon	Pat Green
prince	robin	State Street	town

1. _____   6. _____

2. _____   7. _____

3. _____   8. _____

4. _____   9. _____

5. _____   10. _____

Circle the proper noun in each sentence.

11. I bought apples at Hill's Store.

12. The store is on Baker Street.

13. It is near Stone Library.

14. I gave an apple to Emily Fuller.

Collective Nouns

Some nouns name a group of people, animals, or things. A **collective noun** is a noun that names a group.

Examples:
Our classroom has a <u>group</u> of pictures on the wall.
My <u>family</u> goes to the beach.
I see a <u>flock</u> of birds in the sky.

Find the collective nouns that name a group of people, animals, or things. Write the collective nouns on the lines.

team	mother	boy	teacher
house	herd	bunch	group
flock	baseball	family	apple
book	class	friend	crowd

1. _____   5. _____

2. _____   6. _____

3. _____   7. _____

4. _____   8. _____

Circle the collective noun in each sentence.

9. Our class went on a trip.

10. There are 52 cards in the deck.

11. The band played a song.

12. Chen bought a bunch of bananas.

13. We saw a herd of sheep in the field.

14. A flock of birds landed in the yard.

Name _____ Date _____

Names and Titles of People and Animals

The names of people and animals are proper nouns. The first and last names of a person or animal begin with a capital letter.

The titles of people begin with a capital letter. Most titles end with a period. These are titles of people:

Mr.   Mrs.   Ms.   Miss   Dr.

Examples:
Jack Sprat went to the airport.
Mrs. Sprat is looking for her dog Fluffy.

Write the sentences correctly. Add capital letters where they are needed.

1. Where did jack sprat go?

_____

2. mary saw her friend jill.

_____

3. Did mr. or mrs. sprat go with them?

_____

4. They met ms. muffet along the way.

_____

Write a proper noun to finish each sentence.

5. My dog _____ hid the bone.

6. Teena's cat _____ ate the food.

Names of Special Places

The names of special places are proper nouns. Cities, states, and names of streets begin with a capital letter. The names of countries also begin with a capital letter.

Examples: Jack saw his friends in <u>Miami</u>, <u>Florida</u>.
Their house is at 212 <u>Coconut Drive</u>.
I live in the <u>United States of America</u>.

Write the sentences correctly. Add capital letters where they are needed.

1. They walked along main street.

   _____

2. My uncle drove through indiana and ohio.

   _____

3. We went on a trip to mexico.

   _____

Write a proper noun to finish each sentence.

4. The name of my state is _____.

5. The name of my town is _____.

6. The name of my street is _____.

7. The name of my school is

   _____.

8. _____ is a

pretty place to see in our town.

Days of the Week, Months, and Holidays

The names of the days of the week are proper nouns. They begin with capital letters.

The names of the months are also proper nouns. They begin with capital letters.

The names of holidays are proper nouns, too. Each important word in the name of the holiday begins with a capital letter.

Examples: The man flew in a spaceship on Saturday.
In December, he drives in the snow.
He had a picnic on the Fourth of July.

Complete each sentence. Use the words from the box. Find the day, month, or holiday that begins with the same letter as the underlined word.

Wednesday   Thanksgiving   Saturday   February   July

1. Francis Foley did not walk on _____.

2. He flew in _____.

3. Sometimes he sails on _____.

4. He thinks he will be home for _____.

Write a proper noun to complete each sentence.

5. My birthday is in _____.

6. My favorite day is _____.

7. My favorite holiday is _____.

Singular and Plural Nouns

A noun is a word that names a person, place, or thing.

A noun can tell about more than one person, place, or thing. Add
<u>s</u> to most nouns to make them mean "more than one."

Examples: One <u>girl</u> wears a black hat.
Many <u>boys</u> wear funny masks.

Circle the correct noun to complete each sentence.

1. Two (boy, boys) went out on Halloween.

2. A (girl, girls) walked with them.

3. She wore a black (robe, robes).

4. There were two red (star, stars) on it.

5. It also had one orange (moon, moons).

6. The children walked up to a (house, houses).

7. Then, they knocked on the (door, doors).

8. Will they ask for some (treat, treats)?

9. Then, the children saw two (cat, cats).

10. Two (dog, dogs) ran down the street.

11. An (owl, owls) hooted in the darkness.

12. Many (star, stars) were in the sky.

13. The wind blew through all the (tree, trees).

14. The children clapped their (hand, hands).

Plural Nouns

Add <u>s</u> to most nouns to make them name more than one.

Examples:
one <u>book</u>, four <u>books</u>

Rewrite these nouns to make them name more than one.

1. cap _____

2. chair _____

3. girl _____

4. tree _____

5. flag _____

6. boy _____

Make the noun in ( ) mean more than one. Write the plural noun to complete the sentence.

7. I plant _____ in my garden.
        (seed)

8. I want to grow _____.
        (carrot)

9. I plant some _____, too.
        (pea)

10. My _____ help me.
         (friend)

11. They want to plant _____, too.
         (garden)

Core Skills Language Arts, Grade 2

Unit 1

Name _____ Date _____

More Plural Nouns

> Add <u>es</u> to nouns that end with <u>x</u>, <u>ss</u>, <u>ch</u>, or <u>sh</u> to make them name more than one.
>
> *Examples:*   one <u>fox</u>, ten <u>foxes</u>
> one <u>class</u>, two <u>classes</u>
> one <u>branch</u>, five <u>branches</u>
> one <u>bush</u>, six <u>bushes</u>

Rewrite these nouns to make them name more than one.

1. lunch _____

2. dress _____

3. glass _____

4. dish _____

5. box _____

6. watch _____

Make the noun in ( ) mean more than one. Write the plural noun to complete the sentence.

7. Two _____ walk to the park.
(fox)

8. They sit on two _____.
(bench)

9. Their seats are only _____ apart.
(inch)

10. Then, they take out paints and _____.
(brush)

11. They want to take art _____.
(class)

12. They hope to paint the _____ near the park.
(church)

Name _____ Date _____

Irregular Plural Nouns

Some nouns change spelling to name more than one.

Examples:

    man—men   child—children   tooth—teeth

    woman—women   foot—feet   mouse—mice

Some nouns can name one or more than one.

Examples: one fish—two fish   a deer—three deer

Circle the correct noun in ( ) to complete each sentence.

1. One (woman, women) is working.

2. Many (men, man) are on horses.

3. A (child, children) is wading in the stream.

4. He has no shoes on his (feet, foot).

5. Two (mouses, mice) live in the shed.

Make the noun in ( ) mean more than one. Write the plural noun to complete the sentence.

6. The cats like to chase _____.
                                  (mouse)

7. The little dog has big _____.
                                 (foot)

8. The big dog has little _____.
                                (tooth)

9. Those _____ feed the dogs.
                    (man)

10. The girls feed the _____.
                         (fish)

Name _____ Date _____

Pronouns

A **pronoun** is a word that takes the place of one or more nouns.

Examples:
  The mouse and the lion are friends.
  They are friends.

The pronouns I, we, he, she, it, and they are used in the naming part of a sentence.

  Examples: The mouse helped the lion.
    She helped the lion.

Read the sentences. Think of a pronoun for the underlined words. Write the pronoun on the line.

1. The mouse and I live in the

  woods. _____

2. The mouse fell into the spring.

  _____

3. The lion saw the mouse fall.

  _____

4. The leaf landed in the water.

  _____

5. A hunter spread a net.

  _____

6. The net was for the lion.

  _____

7. The mouse and the lion helped each other.

  _____

8. The mouse and I will always be friends.

  _____

9. The mouse and the lion are happy.

  _____

10. The mouse and I will watch out for the hunter.

  _____

Reflexive Pronouns

> Some pronouns tell about the naming part of a sentence. These pronouns end with <u>self</u> or <u>selves</u>. Pronouns that end with <u>self</u> tell about one person or thing.
>
> *Examples:*   She saw <u>herself</u> in the mirror.
> I wrote the letter <u>myself</u>.
> Dad fixed the car <u>himself</u>.
>
> Pronouns that end with <u>selves</u> tell about more than one person or thing.
>
> *Examples:*   The kittens got out of the box by <u>themselves</u>.
> My sister and I made lunch <u>ourselves</u>.
> Do the work <u>yourselves</u>.

Circle the correct pronoun in ( ) to complete each sentence.

1. The boys made a fort (himself, themselves).

2. I wrote (myself, yourself) a note.

3. My brother and I walk the dog (themselves, ourselves).

4. Mr. Garcia drew the picture (yourself, himself).

Complete each sentence with the correct pronoun from the box.

ourselves   themselves   myself   herself

5. I made _____ a snack.

6. My sister baked the cake _____.

7. The children played by _____.

8. Tom and I washed the dishes _____.

Using I or Me

The word I is always used in the naming part of a sentence.

I is always written with a capital letter.

Example: I go to school.

When you speak of or write about another person and yourself, always name yourself last.

Example: Tina and I are in the same class.

The word me follows a verb, or action word.

Examples: Tina makes me laugh.
The teacher tells Tina and me to be quiet.

Write I or me to complete each sentence correctly.

1. _____ am taking a test.

2. The teacher tells _____ to stop laughing.

3. Mother takes _____ home.

4. _____ have fun with Tina.

Read the sentences. Circle the correct words in ( ) to complete each sentence.

5. (Susan and I, I and Susan) are friends.

6. The teacher tells (Tina and me, me and Tina) to hush.

7. (I and Tina, Tina and I) eat lunch together.

8. Mr. Smith asks (Susan and me, Susan and I) to pass out the papers.

Action Verbs

> An **action verb** is a word that shows action. Verbs tell what a person, place, or thing does.
>
> *Examples:* People <u>drive</u> across the country.
> We <u>walk</u> to school.

Circle the verb in each sentence.

1. Eric runs by Mr. and Mrs. Wilson's house.

2. He kicks a football into the air.

3. The ball breaks the Wilsons' window.

4. Mrs. Wilson looks out the door.

5. Eric runs inside his house.

6. Mother talks to Eric about the window.

7. Mother sends Eric to the Wilsons' house.

8. Eric pays for the window.

Draw a line from each noun to the correct action verb.

Nouns	Verbs
9. The boy	hops.
10. The baby	sing.
11. The rabbit	bark.
12. The birds	cries.
13. The dogs	reads.

Singular Verbs

> Add <u>s</u> to an action verb that tells about one person or thing.
>
> *Examples:*   The boy <u>walks</u> quickly.
> He <u>sees</u> his friends.

Read the sentences. Circle the correct verb in ( ) to complete each sentence.

1. The cat (skip, skips) down the steps.

2. Two cats (play, plays) on the stairs.

3. The boys (hug, hugs) the cat.

4. The cat (purr, purrs) happily.

5. A puppy (bark, barks) at the cat.

6. The boys (hide, hides) from the girls.

7. An ape (wave, waves) to them.

8. The wind (blow, blows) the trees.

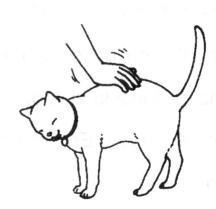

9. My shadow (follow, follows) me.

10. A girl (see, sees) a shadow.

11. Mary (hear, hears) the tree speak.

12. The branches (move, moves) in the wind.

13. An owl (hoot, hoots) in the tree.

14. The girls (take, takes) their treats home.

15. They (eat, eats) some fruit.

Name _____ Date _____

Helping Verbs

A **helping verb** works with the main verb to show action.

Use <u>has</u>, <u>have</u>, and <u>had</u> with other verbs to show action that happened in the past.

Examples: Chen <u>has</u> worked hard.
Brit and Katie <u>have</u> helped.
They <u>had</u> stopped earlier for a snack.

Circle the helping verb in each sentence.

1. Now, we have arrived at the camp.

2. Tom and Bill have unloaded the car.

3. Mr. Green had shopped for food the day before.

4. Bob has gathered firewood.

5. Something strange has happened.

6. A spaceship has landed nearby!

Circle the correct helping verb in ( ) to complete each sentence.

7. We (has, have) built a new playground.

8. Mom and Dad (had, has) sawed the boards before.

9. Donna (has, have) sanded the wood.

10. They (has, have) painted the fence.

11. My brother and I (has, have) raked the leaves.

12. My mother (had, have) forgotten the leaf bags.

Verbs That Do Not Show Action

Some verbs do not show action. They tell about being.

Examples:

A snake <u>is</u> a reptile.   The snake <u>was</u> hungry.

Use <u>am</u> or <u>was</u> with the word I.

Examples:

I <u>am</u> in the tree.   I <u>was</u> under the tree.

Use <u>is</u> or <u>was</u> with one person or thing. Use <u>are</u> or <u>were</u> with more than one person or thing.

Examples:

A lizard <u>is</u> in my garden.   Two turtles <u>were</u> in a box.

Read the sentences. Circle the correct verb in ( ) to complete each sentence.

1. Reptiles (are, is) cold-blooded animals.

2. Some snakes (are, is) dangerous.

3. Many kinds of lizards (were, was) at the zoo.

4. A draco (is, am) a lizard.

5. Crocodiles (are, is) the largest reptiles.

6. The crocodiles (were, was) very noisy.

7. One lizard (is, are) in the box.

8. I (is, am) near the turtle's box.

9. The box (was, were) near the window.

10. The turtle (is, are) sleeping.

Name _____ Date _____

Present-Time Verbs

Present-time verbs tell about action that happens now.

Example: Max and Lisa <u>walk</u> to school.

Add <u>s</u> to an action verb that tells about one person or thing.

Example: Lisa <u>walks</u> to school.

Read the sentences. Circle the correct verb in ( ) to complete each sentence.

1. Max (play, plays) baseball.

2. He (run, runs) fast.

3. The girls (dance, dances) to the music.

4. Some friends (wait, waits) for Max.

5. Lisa (leap, leaps) across the floor.

Finish the story. Add action verbs. You may use words from the box.

sits   stands   asks   takes   walks   dances

Max _____ his sister to her dancing class.

He _____ on a chair to watch. The teacher

_____ him to join the class. First, he

_____ with a girl. Then, he _____

by a wall. Last, he _____ home.

Past-Time Verbs

> Verbs can tell about actions in the past. Form the past tense of most verbs by adding _ed_.
>
> _Example:_
>   Mary Jo <u>planted</u> vegetables yesterday.

Make each sentence tell about the past. Circle the correct verb in ( ) to complete each sentence.

1. Jeff (plays, played) with his sister.

2. The family (visited, visits) Grandmother often.

3. Mary Jo (looks, looked) out the window.

4. Then, she (jumped, jumps) up and down.

5. Grandmother (leans, leaned) back on the pillow.

6. Mary Jo (helps, helped) Grandmother.

7. Grandmother (laughs, laughed) at the baby chicks.

Change each sentence. Make the verb tell about the past. Write the new sentence.

8. The girls play in the park.

    _____

9. They climb over rocks.

    _____

10. Their fathers call to them.

    _____

Irregular Verbs

Some action verbs do not add <u>ed</u> to tell about the past.

Present	Past	Present	Past
go, goes	went	sit, sits	sat
come, comes	came	hide, hides	hid
run, runs	ran	tell, tells	told

Examples: The boys <u>went</u> to sleep.
A dog <u>came</u> to a farm.
The raccoons <u>hid</u> in the woods.

Read the sentences. Circle the correct verb in ( ) to complete each sentence.

1. Three birds (sits, sat) at the feeder.

2. The donkeys (comes, came) to town.

3. Four animals (goes, went) by the house.

4. The rooster and the dog (go, goes) into the kitchen.

5. The friends (hides, hid) in the closet.

6. Marco (tell, told) his friend a secret.

Circle the verb in each sentence. Then, write each verb in the past tense.

7. The man goes to the mill. _____

8. A cat comes to the door. _____

9. The animals sit in the yard. _____

10. They run to the window. _____

Adding ed or ing to Verbs

> To show that something happened in the past, add ed to most verbs.
>
> *Example:*   Don visited Liz yesterday.
>
> To show that something is happening now, you can add ing to most verbs.
>
> *Example:*   Sue is visiting Liz now.

Circle the correct verb in ( ) to complete each sentence.

1. Terry and Joe (played, playing) basketball last week.

2. Jenna (called, calling) to them.

3. She (wanted, wanting) to play, too.

4. The boys (laughed, laughing) at her.

5. But Jenna (jumped, jumping) for the ball.

6. She (played, playing) well.

7. Terry and Joe are not (laughed, laughing) anymore.

8. Now, Jenna is (played, playing) on their team.

9. Everyone is (talked, talking) about all the games they've won.

Add ed or ing to each verb. Then, rewrite each sentence.

10. Carmen help _____ Grandma cook yesterday.

_____

11. Grandma is cook _____ some soup today.

_____

Using Is or Are

Use is and are to tell about something that is happening now.

Use is to tell about one person, place, or thing. Use are to tell about more than one person, place, or thing. Use are with the word you.

Examples: Judy is going.
Lynne and Ed are skating.
The cats are sleeping.
You are lost. Are you scared?

Write is or are to complete each sentence correctly.

1. We _____ going to the park.

2. Al _____ going, too.

3. Kate and Mario _____ running.

4. She _____ the faster runner.

5. Where _____ the twins?

6. They _____ climbing a tree.

7. You _____ going to climb, too.

8. The children _____ having fun.

Write one sentence about a park using is. Then, write one sentence about a park using are.

9. (is) _____

10. (are) _____

Using <u>Was</u> or <u>Were</u>

Use <u>was</u> and <u>were</u> to tell about something that happened in the past.

Use <u>was</u> to tell about one person, place, or thing. Use <u>were</u> to tell about more than one person, place, or thing. Use <u>were</u> with the word <u>you</u>.

Examples: My bat <u>was</u> on the step.
Ten people <u>were</u> there.
You <u>were</u> late. <u>Were</u> you home?

Circle the correct verb in ( ) to complete each sentence.

1. The children (was, were) indoors while it rained.

2. José (was, were) reading a book.

3. Scott and Jay (was, were) playing checkers.

4. Ann, Roy, and Jami (was, were) playing cards.

5. Sara and Tara (was, were) talking.

6. Nick (was, were) beating a drum.

7. I (was, were) drawing pictures.

8. You (was, were) dancing.

Write one sentence about a rainy day using <u>was</u>. Then, write one sentence about a rainy day using <u>were</u>.

9. (was) _____

10. (were) _____

Using <u>See</u>, <u>Sees</u>, or <u>Saw</u>

Use <u>see</u> or <u>sees</u> to tell what is happening now. Use <u>see</u> with the words <u>you</u> and <u>I</u>. Use <u>saw</u> to tell what happened in the past.

Examples: One boy <u>sees</u> a dog. Two boys <u>see</u> a dog.
I <u>see</u> a dog. Do you <u>see</u> a dog?
Justin <u>saw</u> Natalie last week.

Write <u>see</u>, <u>sees</u>, or <u>saw</u> to complete each sentence correctly.

1. Mike _____ his friend Lori now.

2. He _____ her last Monday.

3. Lori _____ Mike paint now.

4. My dad _____ Mike paint now, too.

5. Mike _____ a beautiful sky last night.

6. He _____ pink in the sky on Sunday.

7. Grandpa and I _____ some trains now.

8. We _____ many trains on my last birthday.

9. We _____ old and new trains last winter.

10. Today, I can _____ the train show.

11. Last week, we _____ Lee.

12. Lee _____ my painting now.

Using <u>Run</u>, <u>Runs</u>, or <u>Ran</u>

Use <u>run</u> or <u>runs</u> to tell what is happening now. Use <u>run</u> with the words <u>you</u> and <u>I</u>. Use <u>ran</u> to tell what happened in the past.

Examples: One horse <u>runs</u>. Two horses <u>run</u>.
I <u>run</u> in the park. Do you <u>run</u>?
Yesterday, we <u>ran</u> to the park.

Write <u>run</u>, <u>runs</u>, or <u>ran</u>. Then, rewrite each sentence.

1. Horses _____ wild long ago.

_____

2. A horse can _____ ten miles every day.

_____

3. Can you _____ as fast as a horse?

_____

4. Mandy _____ in a race last week.

_____

5. Carl _____ home from school now.

_____

6. Now, Mandy _____ after Carl.

_____

7. How far can you _____?

_____

Using Give, Gives, or Gave

Use give or gives to tell what is happening now. Use give with the words you and I. Use gave to tell what happened in the past.

Examples: One student gives a gift. Two students give a gift.
I give a gift. Do you give one?
Jenna gave me a present yesterday.

Read the sentences. Circle the correct verb in ( ) to complete each sentence.

1. Can you (give, gives, gave) the animals some food?

2. Sandi (give, gives, gave) them water yesterday.

3. Juan (give, gives, gave) the chickens corn now.

4. Chickens (give, gives, gave) us eggs to eat yesterday.

5. We (give, gives, gave) the kittens some milk last night.

6. Who (give, gives, gave) hay to the cow then?

7. Our cow (give, gives, gave) us milk yesterday.

8. I (give, gives, gave) food to the pigs last Monday.

Write three sentences about gifts using give, gives, and gave.

9. (give) _____

10. (gives) _____

11. (gave) _____

Using <u>Do</u> or <u>Does</u>

Use <u>does</u> to tell about one person, place, or thing.
Use <u>do</u> to tell about more than one person, place,
or thing. Also, use <u>do</u> with the words <u>you</u> and <u>I</u>.

Examples: William <u>does</u> the work.
They <u>do</u> the work.
I <u>do</u> the work. You <u>do</u> the work.

Write <u>do</u> or <u>does</u> to complete each sentence correctly.

1. We _____ a lot of work in the house.

2. My dad _____ all the dishes.

3. My mom _____ the windows.

4. My sister _____ the sweeping.

5. My grandma _____ the sewing.

6. I _____ the floor.

7. My little brother _____ the dusting.

8. I _____ not cook dinner.

9. My big sister _____ her homework.

10. We all _____ some work in our house.

**Write one sentence about yourself using <u>do</u>. Then, write one
sentence about a friend using <u>does</u>.**

11. _____

12. _____

Using <u>Has</u>, <u>Have</u>, or <u>Had</u>

Use <u>has</u> to tell about one person, place, or thing. Use <u>have</u> to tell about more than one person, place, or thing. Use <u>have</u> with the words <u>you</u> and <u>I</u>. Use <u>had</u> to tell about the past.

Examples: Jesse <u>has</u> a bird.
Cars <u>have</u> tires.
You <u>have</u> new shoes. I <u>have</u> fun.
My dogs <u>had</u> fleas. Bill <u>had</u> a cat last year.

Circle the correct verb in ( ) to complete each sentence.

1. My brother (has, have, had) a pet fish last year.

2. Now, Dan (has, have, had) a pet mouse.

3. The pets (has, have, had) good homes now.

4. I (has, have, had) a football now.

5. Now, Dana (has, have, had) a pair of roller skates, too.

6. Yesterday, Dawn (has, have, had) a full balloon.

7. Now, the balloon (has, have, had) a hole in it.

8. She (has, have, had) the money to buy another balloon today.

Write <u>has</u>, <u>have</u>, or <u>had</u> to complete each sentence correctly.

9. You _____ many friends now.

10. Your friends _____ fun together last Saturday.

11. Last week, I _____ supper with Eric.

12. Now, he _____ supper with me.

Adjectives

An **adjective** is a describing word. A describing word tells about a noun.

Example: The <u>old</u> woman walked home.

Describing words can tell about color or size.

Example: <u>Red</u> flowers grow in the <u>small</u> garden.

Describing words can tell about shape.

Example: The house has a <u>square</u> window.

Describing words can tell how something feels, tastes, sounds, or smells.

Example: The flowers have a <u>sweet</u> smell.

Finish the sentences. Add describing words from the box.

round	long	brown	tiny	pink	juicy

1. The woman puts on a _____ bonnet.

2. She walks down a _____ road.

3. Some _____ squirrels run by.

4. A man gives her a _____ orange.

5. The orange is _____.

6. Do you see a _____ bone in the yard?

Adjectives, part 2

> Adjectives are describing words. Describing words can describe feelings.
>
> *Examples:*   The woman was <u>surprised</u>.
>   She was <u>happy</u>.
>
> Describing words can also tell how many.
>
> *Example:*   She picked <u>four</u> flowers.
>
> Some describing words that tell how many do not tell exact numbers.
>
> *Examples:*   There are <u>many</u> roses in the garden.
>   <u>Some</u> grass grows here.

Finish the sentences. Add describing words from the box.

happy   some   hungry   tired   three   sleepy   one   many

1. The woman was _____ from walking so far.

2. She was _____ to be home.

3. First, she put _____ flowers in a vase.

4. Next, she put _____ cup of water in the vase.

5. She was _____ and wanted to eat.

6. Then, she ate _____ soup.

7. She also had _____ crackers.

8. Last, the woman was _____ and went to bed.

Adjectives That Compare

Add <u>er</u> to most describing words when they are used to compare two things.

Example: This tree is <u>taller</u> than that one.

Add <u>est</u> to most describing words when they are used to compare more than two things.

Example: The sequoia tree is the <u>tallest</u> tree of all.

Read the chart. Fill in the missing describing words.

1.	long	longer	longest
2.	bright		brightest
3.	tall	taller	
4.		faster	fastest

Circle the correct describing word in ( ) to complete each sentence.

5. That tree trunk is (thick, thicker) than this one.

6. The giant sequoia is the (bigger, biggest) living thing of all.

7. The stump of a giant sequoia is (wider, widest) than my room.

8. These trees are the (older, oldest) of all.

32

Using <u>A</u> or <u>An</u>

<u>A</u> and <u>an</u> are called **articles**. They are special adjectives.

Use <u>an</u> before words that begin with a vowel sound. The vowels are <u>a</u>, <u>e</u>, <u>i</u>, <u>o</u>, and <u>u</u>.

Use <u>a</u> before words that begin with a consonant sound.

Examples: <u>an</u> apple, <u>an</u> egg
<u>a</u> car, <u>a</u> skate

Choose the correct article. Write <u>a</u> or <u>an</u> before each word.

1. _____ arm

2. _____ dog

3. _____ hat

4. _____ ant

5. _____ cat

6. _____ elf

7. _____ ear

8. _____ office

9. _____ fire

10. _____ cow

11. _____ uncle

12. _____ tree

13. _____ inch

14. _____ ax

15. _____ top

16. _____ boat

17. _____ duck

18. _____ eagle

Write <u>a</u> or <u>an</u> to complete each sentence correctly.

19. Randy put _____ apple in my box.

20. Victor has _____ old bike.

21. Linda has two balls and _____ bat.

22. I have _____ sweet apple.

Adverbs

An **adverb** tells more about the action word or verb in a sentence. Adverbs tell how, when, or where. Some adverbs end with ly.

Examples: Ming quickly solved the problem. (how)
Caden talked loudly. (how)
It will start raining soon. (when)
Donna's birthday is tomorrow. (when)
Carlos played outside. (where)
The cat jumped down from the tree. (where)

Finish the sentences. Add adverbs from the box.

loudly	everywhere	quietly	quickly
outside	tomorrow	later	inside

1. Gina was reading _____ by herself.

2. Gina heard a noise and looked _____.

3. An orange cat meowed _____ on the roof.

4. She ran _____ down the stairs and out the door.

5. She went back _____ to get her camera.

6. She looked _____ for her camera.

7. Gina _____ found her camera in her desk.

8. She will tell her friend Sue what she saw _____.

Adverbs, part 2

Adverbs describe the verb in a sentence.

An adverb can tell <u>how</u> something happens.

Examples: Jen sang <u>softly</u>.
              <u>Suddenly</u>, the dog barked.

An adverb can tell <u>when</u> something happens.

Examples: Pete called <u>today</u>.
              The bus comes <u>early</u>.

An adverb can tell <u>where</u> something happens.

Examples: Tino put the book <u>there</u>.
              The birds are <u>high</u> in the air.

Finish the sentences. Add adverbs from the box.

| down   neatly   early   up   Later   today   there   over   Soon |

1. Lisa will wake up _____ .

2. Lisa and Mike are going to the beach _____ .

3. They will see the sun come _____ .

4. Mike plays in the sand _____ .

5. He packs the sand _____ in a bucket.

6. He turns the bucket _____ to make a castle.

7. _____, Lisa helps Mike.

8. _____, they will swim.

9. Waves crash _____ on the beach.

Using Adjectives or Adverbs

An adjective describes a noun. It tells more about a person, animal, place, or thing.

Examples: The <u>black</u> kitten is <u>small</u>.
It plays with a <u>round</u> ball of string.

An adverb describes a verb. It tells how, when, or where something happens.

Examples: The kitten <u>quickly</u> swats the ball.
<u>Then</u>, she chases it.

Circle the correct adjective or adverb in ( ) to complete each sentence.

1. The bus drives (slow, slowly).

2. We pass the (slow, slowly) bus.

3. She has a (small, there) dog.

4. The dog barks (loudly, soft).

5. My teacher sits at a (here, big) desk.

6. He is (hungry, often), and he wants to eat.

7. He will eat lunch (large, now).

Write one sentence about an animal using an adjective to tell about the animal. Then, write one sentence using an adverb to tell how, when, or where the animal does something.

8. _____

9. _____

Name _____ Date _____

Using Adjectives or Adverbs, part 2

> Use an adjective to tell about a person, animal, place, or thing.
>
> *Examples:*   I have a <u>new</u> friend.
>   She is <u>tall</u>.
>
> Use an adverb to tell about how, when, or where.
>
> *Examples:*   <u>Today</u>, I made a friend.
>   We played <u>happily</u> <u>outside</u>.

Circle the correct adjective or adverb in ( ) to complete each sentence.

1. The boy cried (sadly, sad).

2. The (sadly, sad) boy wanted candy.

3. The (quick, quickly) fox ran away.

4. The fox lives in a (quiet, quietly) den.

Finish the story. Use adjectives and adverbs from the box.

| happy   colorful   yesterday   over   carefully   new   blue |

Karen went to the library _____. She saw a

_____ book. She opened the book

_____. The book had _____ pictures

of bugs. She saw a dragonfly with _____ wings. Karen

took the book _____ to the desk. Her mom helped her

check it out. Karen is _____ about the book.

Unit 2: Sentences
Complete Sentences

A **sentence** is a group of words that tells or asks something. It is a complete thought. Every sentence begins with a capital letter. Every sentence ends with a punctuation mark.

Examples: Friends play.
           Cars go fast.

Write yes if the group of words is a sentence. Write no if the group of words is not a sentence.

_____ **1.** A long time ago.

_____ **2.** The class went to the park.

_____ **3.** Near the tree.

_____ **4.** Ten children played.

_____ **5.** Mark hit the ball.

_____ **6.** A dog chased the ball.

_____ **7.** Bill and Tom.

_____ **8.** Ran and played all day.

_____ **9.** Everyone had fun.

_____ **10.** Jan lost a new red shoe.

_____ **11.** We ate lunch.

_____ **12.** Too hot for us.

_____ **13.** The boys and girls talked.

Complete Sentences, part 2

Remember that a sentence tells a complete thought.

Examples: Mari caught the ball.
Chad read a book.

Draw lines between the groups of words to make sentences.

1.	Mrs. Brown	live in our building.
2.	Our building	is made of wood.
3.	Four families	lives on my street.

4.	Our class	was climbing the tree.
5.	Jennifer	went on a picnic.
6.	The sun	shines all day.

7.	Corn and beans	fed the baby goat.
8.	The wagon	has a broken wheel.
9.	The mother goat	grow on a farm.

10.	The boat	sailed in strong winds.
11.	The fisher	were sold in the store.
12.	Some of the fish	caught seven fish.

13.	Our team	hit the ball a lot.
14.	Our batters	won ten games.
15.	The ballpark	was full of fans.

Write a sentence about your birthday.

16. _____

Sentence Parts

Every sentence has two parts. The **naming part** tells who or what the sentence is about. The naming part is called the subject.

The **action part** tells something about the naming part. The action part is called the predicate.

A naming part and an action part make a complete thought.

Examples:	**Naming Part**	**Action Part**
	Sara	plants some seeds.

Each group of words needs a naming part or an action part. Add words to make each group of words a complete sentence.

1. John _____.

2. Sara _____.

3. _____ need sunshine and rain.

4. The flower seeds _____.

5. John and Sara _____.

6. _____ looks at the flower.

7. _____ grow in the garden.

8. The flowers _____.

9. _____ bloom in the spring.

10. _____ are my favorite flowers.

11. The butterflies _____.

12. _____ makes the flowers grow.

Naming Part of Sentences

The naming part of a sentence tells who or what the sentence is about.

Examples: <u>Three mice</u> run away.
<u>The cat</u> plays with a ball.

Circle the naming part of each sentence.

1. My family and I live on a busy street.

2. Sami Harper found a bird.

3. Miss Jenkins drives very slowly.

4. Mr. Chang walks his dog.

5. Henry throws to his dog.

6. Mr. Byrne cuts his grass.

7. Mrs. Lee picks up her children.

8. Mr. and Mrs. Diaz shop for food.

9. Jeanine plays in the park.

10. Mr. Wolf brings the mail.

11. Amy Taft brings the paper.

12. Mr. Dowd cooks dinner.

13. Mrs. Clark washes her windows.

14. Carolyn and Alberto plant flower seeds.

15. Julie waters the garden.

Action Part of Sentences

The action part of a sentence tells what someone or something does.

Examples: Three mice <u>run away</u>.
The cat <u>plays with a ball</u>.

Choose an action part from the box to complete each sentence. Write it on the line.

barks   buzz   fly   hops   moo   cluck   quack   roar

1. Robins and blackbirds _____.

2. Yellow bees _____.

3. My little dog _____.

4. Mother Duck and her babies _____.

5. A rabbit with big feet _____.

6. Angry lions _____.

7. All the cows on the farm _____.

8. Chickens _____.

Write a sentence about an animal that you like. Circle the naming part. Underline the action part.

_____

_____

42

Word Order in Sentences

> Words in a sentence must be in an order that makes sense.
>
> *Examples:*   Grandpa plays baseball.
>   My sister writes stories.

Write each group of words in an order that makes sense. Be sure to put a period at the end of each sentence.

1. brother My apples eats

_____

2. drinks Elizabeth milk

_____

3. butter peanut Kim likes

_____

4. Justin bread wants

_____

5. corn plants Chris

_____

6. a fish Chang caught

_____

7. breakfast cooks Dad

_____

Telling Sentences and Asking Sentences

A **telling sentence** is a group of words that tells something. A telling sentence is also called a statement.

Examples: I fed my pony.
Ponies like to run and play.

An **asking sentence** is a group of words that asks a question. You can answer an asking sentence. An asking sentence is also called a question.

Examples: How old are you?
Where do you live?

Write telling on the line before the group of words if it is a telling sentence. Write asking on the line before the group of words if it is an asking sentence. Leave the line blank if the group of words is not a sentence.

_____ **1.** Josh loves his pony.

_____ **2.** His name is Zip.

_____ **3.** Do you like horses?

_____ **4.** Fast horses.

_____ **5.** Zip can run fast.

_____ **6.** Over the hill.

_____ **7.** He eats apples.

_____ **8.** Do you eat apples?

_____ **9.** Zip has soft hair.

Name _____ Date _____

Kinds of Sentences

A **statement** is a sentence that tells something. It begins with a capital letter. It ends with a period (**.**).

Example: John gives some seeds to Sara.

A **question** is a sentence that asks something. It begins with a capital letter. It ends with a question mark (**?**).

Example: Will Sara plant seeds?

An **exclamation** is a sentence that shows strong feeling. It begins with a capital letter. It ends with an exclamation point (**!**).

Example: What a fine garden John has!

Read the sentences. Write <u>statement</u> for a telling sentence. Write <u>question</u> for an asking sentence. Write <u>exclamation</u> for a sentence that shows strong feeling.

_____ **1.** John was in his garden.

_____ **2.** Who came walking by?

_____ **3.** Sara stopped to look at the garden.

_____ **4.** What did Sara do?

_____ **5.** Sara read a story to her seeds.

_____ **6.** Did Sara do anything else?

_____ **7.** Poor Sara fell asleep in her garden!

_____ **8.** The seeds started to grow.

_____ **9.** What makes seeds grow?

_____ **10.** Sara works so hard!

Kinds of Sentences, part 2

> Use a statement to tell something. End a statement with a period.
>
> Use a question to ask something. End a question with a question mark.
>
> Use an exclamation to show strong feeling. End an exclamation with an exclamation point.

Make each sentence a statement. Be sure to use the correct end mark.

1. My favorite animal is _____

2. My favorite food is _____

3. My favorite color is _____

Make each sentence a question. Be sure to use the correct end mark.

4. What is _____

5. Where _____

6. Why _____

Make each sentence an exclamation. Be sure to use the correct end mark.

7. I love _____

8. It's so _____

Joining Sentences

A writer can join two short sentences.

If the naming parts of two sentences are the same, then the action parts can be joined. Use the word <u>and</u> to join the sentences.

Example:
John planted seeds. John worked in his garden.
John planted seeds <u>and</u> worked in his garden.

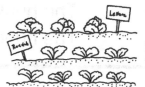

How to Join Sentences

1. Look for sentences that have the same naming part.

2. Write the naming part.

3. Look for different action parts. Use the word <u>and</u> to join them.

Use the word <u>and</u> to join each pair of sentences. Write the new sentences.

1. John gave seeds to Sara. John told her to plant them.

   _____

2. Sara planted the seeds. Sara looked at the ground.

   _____

3. Sara sang songs to her seeds. Sara read stories to them.

   _____

4. The rain fell on the seeds. The rain helped them grow.

   _____

Joining Sentences, part 2

If the action parts of two sentences are the same, then the naming parts can be joined. Use the word <u>and</u> to join the sentences.

Example:
The hunter stopped at the house. The bear stopped at the house.
The hunter <u>and</u> the bear stopped at the house.

How to Join Sentences

1. Look for sentences that have the same action part.

2. Join the naming parts. Use the word <u>and</u>.

3. Add the action part.

Use the word <u>and</u> to join each pair of sentences. Write the new sentences.

1. The farmer stood in the doorway. His family stood in the doorway.

   _____

2. The hunter stayed with the family. The bear stayed with the family.

   _____

3. The mice ran out the door. The children ran out the door.

   _____

4. The hunter went home. The bear went home.

   _____

Joining Sentences, part 3

A writer can join two sentences that are closely related. Use a comma and the word <u>and</u> to join the sentences.

Example:
Joe rakes the leaves. Meg puts them in bags.
Joe rakes the leaves, and Meg puts them in bags.

How to Join Sentences

1. Look for sentences that are closely related.

2. Use a comma and the word <u>and</u> to join the sentences.

3. Read the sentence aloud to make sure the sentence makes sense.

Join the two sentences to make one sentence. Use a comma and the word <u>and</u>. Write the new sentences.

1. Vince has a ball. I have a bat.

_____

2. Mom drives a car. Dad drives a truck.

_____

3. Jim has a dog. Amy has a cat.

_____

4. Mr. Lopez teaches art. Mrs. Moore teaches science.

_____

Making Sentences More Interesting

A writer can join sentences by adding details from closely related sentences.

Example: Tran sends a card. The card is a birthday card. Tran sends the card in the mail.
Tran sends a <u>birthday</u> card <u>in the mail</u>.

A writer can also change the order of words.

Example: Lara painted that picture on the wall.
That picture on the wall was painted by Lara.

Join the sentences to make one sentence by adding details.

1. The bear went to his den. The bear was brown. The den was large.

The _____ bear went to his _____ den.

2. The bear was hungry. The bear ate berries. The bear ate fish.

The _____ bear ate _____

and _____ .

Write a new sentence by changing the order of words.

3. The bear turned over the trash can.

The trash can was _____ by

_____ .

4. The loud noise woke the campers. The campers were sleeping.

The _____ campers were woken by

_____ .

Adding Describing Words to Sentences

> A good writer adds describing words to sentences to give a clear picture. The words can tell about nouns or actions.
>
> *Example:*
>   The moth landed on a clover.
>   The <u>black</u> moth landed <u>gently</u> on a <u>white</u> clover.

How to Add Describing Words to Sentences

1. Look for sentences that do not give your reader a clear picture.

2. Think of words that tell more about what things look like or how they happen.

3. Add the describing words to the sentences.

Add describing words to these sentences. Write the new sentences.

1. The clown wears a hat.

   _____

2. A lion jumps through a hoop.

   _____

3. A monkey rides on an elephant.

   _____

4. A butterfly flew into the tent.

   _____

Beginning Sentences in Different Ways

A good writer should not begin every sentence with the same noun. Sometimes the words <u>he</u>, <u>she</u>, <u>I</u>, <u>we</u>, and <u>they</u> are used in place of nouns.

Example:
Ant climbed down a branch. Ant was thirsty.
<u>She</u> tried to get a drink.

How to Begin Sentences in Different Ways

1. Look for sentences that begin with the same noun.

2. Use the word <u>he</u>, <u>she</u>, <u>I</u>, <u>we</u>, or <u>they</u> in place of the noun.

3. Write the new sentence.

Change the way some of these sentences begin. Begin some of them with He, She, I, We, or They. Write the new sentences.

1. The ant climbed down a blade of grass. The ant fell into the spring.

_____

2. The bird pulled off a leaf. The bird let the leaf fall into the water.

_____

3. The hunter saw a lion. The hunter spread his net.

_____

4. The lion and I live in the woods. The lion and I are friends.

_____

Writing Clear Sentences

A good writer uses exact verbs. These are verbs that give a clear picture of an action.

Example: Spaceships <u>go</u> to the moon.
Spaceships <u>zoom</u> to the moon.

How to Use Exact Verbs in Sentences

1. Picture the action. Think about what a person or thing is doing.

2. Choose an action verb that tells exactly what the person or thing is doing.

3. Use the action verb in a sentence.

Think of a more exact verb for each underlined verb. Write the new word on the line.

1. People <u>walk</u> to work.   _____

2. Trains <u>move</u> along the tracks.   _____

3. We <u>ride</u> our bicycles.   _____

4. Fast cars <u>go</u> up the road.   _____

5. The airplane <u>flies</u> in the sky.   _____

6. A man <u>runs</u> around the park.   _____

7. The children <u>walk</u> to school.   _____

8. A bus <u>goes</u> down the highway.   _____

9. The boat <u>moves</u> along the shore.   _____

Unit 2
Core Skills Language Arts, Grade 2

Unit 3: Mechanics
Writing Names of People

Each word of a person's name begins with a capital letter.

Examples: Mary Ann Miller
Mark Twain
Grandma Moses

Rewrite the names. Use capital letters where they are needed.

1. eric carle   _____

2. beverly cleary   _____

3. diane dillon   _____

4. alicia acker   _____

5. ezra jack keats   _____

Circle the letters that should be capital letters.

6. Today, mother called grandma.

7. We will see grandma and grandpa at the party.

8. Will uncle carlos and aunt kathy be there, too?

Rewrite the sentences. Use capital letters where they are needed.

9. mario martinez told me a story.

_____

10. ichiro and I played ball.

_____

Writing Initials

> An **initial** stands for a person's name. It is a capital letter with a period **(.)** after it.
>
> *Examples:* Steven Bell Mathis = Steven **B**. Mathis or **S. B.** Mathis or **S. B. M.**

Write the initials of each name.

1. Clara Delrio _____   5. Keiko Senda _____

2. Carrie Anne Collier _____   6. Terri Lynn Turner _____

3. Marcus Brown _____   7. Isaiah Bradley _____

4. Michael Tond _____   8. Cata Lil Walker _____

Rewrite the names. Use initials for the names that are underlined.

9. <u>Joan</u> <u>Walsh</u> <u>Anglund</u>   11. <u>Arturo</u> Martinez

_____   _____

10. <u>Lee</u> <u>Bennett</u> Hopkins   12. Patricia <u>Ann</u> Rosen

_____   _____

Rewrite the sentences. Be sure to write the initials correctly.

13. The box was for m s mills.

_____

14. d e ellis sent it to her.

_____

Writing Titles of Respect

Begin a **title of respect** with a capital letter.

End <u>Mr.</u>, <u>Mrs.</u>, <u>Ms.</u>, and <u>Dr.</u> with a period. They are short forms, or abbreviations, of longer words.

Do not end <u>Miss</u> with a period.

Examples: Mr. George Selden
              Dr. Martin Luther King
              Miss Jane Pittman

Rewrite the names correctly. Place periods and capital letters where they are needed.

1. mrs ruth scott   _____

2. mr kurt wiese   _____

3. miss e garcia   _____

4. ms carol baylor   _____

5. mr and mrs h cox   _____

6. dr s tomas rios   _____

Rewrite the sentences correctly. Place periods and capital letters where they are needed.

7. mrs h stone is here to see dr brooks.

_____

8. mr f green and ms miller are not here.

_____

Name _____ Date _____

Writing Names of Places

The names of cities, states, and countries begin with a capital letter.

The names of streets, parks, lakes, rivers, and schools begin with a capital letter.

The abbreviations of the words <u>street</u>, <u>road</u>, and <u>drive</u> in a place name begin with a capital letter and end with a period.

Examples: Reno, Nevada
Canada
Parker School
Central Park
Red River
Dove Rd. (Road = Rd.)

Rewrite the sentences. Use capital letters where they are needed.

1. James lives in dayton, ohio.

_____

2. His house is on market st.

_____

3. I think thomas park is in this town.

_____

4. We went to mathis lake for a picnic.

_____

5. Is main street far away?

_____

Writing Names of Days and Months

The names of days of the week begin with a capital letter.

The names of the months begin with a capital letter.

Examples: Monday, Friday   April, February

The abbreviations of the days of the week begin with a capital letter. They end with a period.

The abbreviations of the months begin with a capital letter. They end with a period. The names May, June, and July are not usually abbreviated.

Examples: Sun., Mon., Tues., Wed., Thurs., Fri., Sat.
Jan., Feb., Mar., Apr., Aug., Sept., Oct., Nov., Dec.

Write the name of a day or month to complete each sentence.

1. The day after Sunday is _____.

2. The day before Saturday is _____.

3. Valentine's Day is in _____.

4. A month in the summer is _____.

5. Thanksgiving Day is in _____.

Write the correct abbreviation for each day or month. Be sure to end the abbreviation with a period.

6. Tuesday _____   **9.** Saturday _____

7. Thursday _____   **10.** January _____

8. December _____   **11.** September _____

Writing Names of Holidays

Each important word in the name of a
holiday begins with a capital letter.

Examples: Earth Day
                Memorial Day
                Fourth of July

Write the holiday names correctly.

1. new year's day _____

2. mothers' day _____

3. independence day _____

4. labor day _____

5. presidents' day _____

6. thanksgiving day _____

7. veterans day _____

Rewrite each sentence correctly.

8. valentine's day is in February.

_____

9. boxing day is a British holiday.

_____

10. father's day is in June.

_____

Writing Product Names

> The brand names of **products** (things you buy) start with a capital letter.
>
> *Examples:*   Kleenex
>   Coke
>   Super Clean soap
>
> Do not use a capital letter for common nouns.
>
> *Examples:*   a box of tissues
>   soda

Write the product names correctly.

1. pepsi

_____

2. lucky charms

_____

3. cheerios

_____

4. ford focus

_____

5. xbox

_____

6. barbie

_____

Rewrite each sentence correctly.

7. Tonya wears nike tennis shoes.

_____

8. Do you like coke or pepsi better?

_____

Name _____ Date _____

Writing Titles of Books, Stories, and Poems

Begin the first word and last word in the title of a book with a capital letter. All other words begin with a capital letter except unimportant words. Some unimportant words are <u>a</u>, <u>an</u>, <u>the</u>, <u>of</u>, <u>with</u>, <u>for</u>, <u>at</u>, <u>in</u>, and <u>on</u>. Draw a line under the title of a book.

Examples: <u>The Snowy Day</u>   <u>Storm at Sea</u>

Begin the first word, last word, and all important words in the title of a story or poem with a capital letter. Put quotation marks (" ") around the title of a story or poem.

Examples: "Jonas and the Monster" (story)
            "Something Is Out There" (poem)

Write these book titles correctly. Be sure to underline the title of a book.

1. best friends

_____

2. the biggest bear

_____

3. rabbits on roller skates

_____

4. down on the sunny farm

_____

Read the sentences. Circle the letters that should be capital letters.

5. My favorite poem is called "we bees."

6. I read a story called "the dancing pony" last week.

7. Robert Louis Stevenson wrote a poem called "my shadow."

8. Lori wrote a story named "my summer on the farm."

Using Spelling Patterns

A good writer spells words correctly. Sometimes a sound in English can have different spellings. Here are some different ways to spell vowel sounds.

Long a	Long e	Long i	Long o
cake	feet	dime	coat
rain	heat	cry	sold
day	baby	pie	bone
	babies	high	show

Some consonants can also be spelled different ways.

Examples:

/j/ as in jump	jar	bridge	page
/k/ as in kitten	keep	pack	come
/z/ as in zebra	zip	buzz	nose

Circle the word in ( ) that is spelled correctly.

1. Her (phone, fone) rang loudly.

2. The (chickens, chikens) like to eat bugs.

3. The (train, trane) stops here every hour.

Each sentence has three spelling errors. Rewrite each sentence correctly.

4. The sweet shop sells fudj, kakes, and cookees.

_____

5. I wore a yello cote in the rane.

_____

Beginning Sentences

Begin the first word of a sentence with a capital letter.

Examples: The garden is very pretty.
                 Flowers grow there.
                 What kind of flowers do you see?

Rewrite these sentences. Begin each sentence with a capital letter.

1. there are many kinds of gardens.

_____

2. vegetables grow in some gardens.

_____

3. you can find gardens in parks.

_____

4. i like to work in the garden.

_____

5. deb likes to play ball.

_____

6. her ball is red.

_____

7. jet wants to play.

_____

Ending Sentences

Put a **period (.)** at the end of a sentence that tells something.

Examples: Patty is my friend.
We play together.

Put a **question mark (?)** at the end of a sentence that asks something.

Examples: Is he your brother?
Do you have a sister?

Rewrite these telling sentences. Use capital letters and periods where they are needed.

1. patty played on the baseball team

_____

2. patty hit two home runs

_____

3. she caught the ball, too

_____

Rewrite these asking sentences. Use capital letters and question marks where they are needed.

4. what time is it

_____

5. is it time for lunch

_____

Periods

> Use a **period (.)** at the end of a statement.
>
> *Example:*   I like to read books about frogs.
>
> Put a period at the end of most titles of people.
>
> *Example:*   Mr. Arnold Lobel wrote the book.
>
> These are titles of people.
>
>   Mr.   Mrs.   Ms.   Dr.   Miss

Correct the sentences. Add periods where they are needed.

1. John has a nice garden

2. The flowers are pretty

3. John gave Sara some seeds

4. Sara will plant them in the ground

5. Little green plants will grow

6. Ms Sara thought the seeds were afraid.

7. Mr John told Sara not to worry.

8. Mrs Jones told Sara to wait a few days.

9. Sara showed her garden to Dr Dewey.

10. Ms Babbitt thinks Sara has a nice garden.

Question Marks, Exclamation Points, and Apostrophes

Use a **question mark (?)** at the end of a question.

Example: Who are you?

Use an **exclamation point (!)** at the end of an exclamation.

Example: Leave me alone!

Use an **apostrophe (')** to show that one or more letters have been left out in a contraction.

Example: His parents didn't take Stewart anywhere.

Finish the sentences correctly. Add question marks and exclamation points where they are needed.

1. Stewart just does not care

2. Would you rather stay here

3. Does Stewart care about anything

4. Yes, indeed he cares

Circle the correct contraction in ( ) to complete each sentence.

5. Stewart said, "I (dont, don't) care!"

6. "(Ill, I'll) get you," said the bear.

7. Stewart (didn't, didnt) want to stay with the bear.

8. The bear said, "(We'll, Well) be best friends!"

Name _____ Date _____

Using Apostrophes in Contractions

A **contraction** is a word made by joining two words. An **apostrophe** (') shows where a letter or letters are left out.

Examples: is not = isn't   did not = didn't
do not = don't   are not = aren't

Draw a line from the two words to the contraction.

1. were not   hasn't

2. was not   haven't

3. has not   wasn't

4. have not   weren't

5. did not   aren't

6. are not   didn't

Write each contraction as two words.

7. isn't _____ _____

8. don't _____ _____

9. wasn't _____ _____

10. hasn't _____ _____

11. didn't _____ _____

12. hadn't _____ _____

13. doesn't _____ _____

14. aren't _____ _____

Write a contraction for the words in ( ).

15. Today (is not) _____ a good day.

16. I (do not) _____ have my lunch.

17. I (did not) _____ finish my work.

Using Apostrophes in Possessives

An apostrophe can be used to show who owns or has something. Add an **apostrophe** (') and the letter **s** (**'s**) to the end of a noun to show ownership.

Examples: the dog's collar   the mouse's tail
              Jack's book   a baby's crib

Add an apostrophe and s to show ownership.

1. the house of a friend   a friend   house

2. a toy that Mike has   Mike   toy

3. the bucket of the farmer   the farmer   bucket

4. the tires on the car   the car   tires

5. a picture that belongs to Val   Val   picture

6. a bike that Judy has   Judy   bike

7. the nest the bird has   the bird   nest

Rewrite each group of words to show ownership. Use 's.

8. the bread from the bakery

_____

9. the desk of Mr. Smith

_____

10. the pen that Ally has

_____

Commas

Use a **comma (,)** between the name of a city and a state.

Examples: Toledo, Ohio
Albany, New York

Use a comma (,) between the day and the year in a date.

Examples: July 4, 1776
November 1, 2014

Use a comma (,) after the greeting and after the closing in a letter.

Examples: Dear Mom and Dad,
Your friend,

Read Mary Jane's letter to Grandmother. Put commas where they are needed.

June 8 2013

Dear Grandmother

    I hope you are feeling better. Mom and I went shopping yesterday. We found a pretty new jacket for you. The tag says it comes from Chicago Illinois. I hope you like the jacket. Please write to me soon.

Love

Mary Jane

Using Commas in Place Names

> Put a comma between the name of a city and its state. Names of cities and states begin with a capital letter.
>
> *Examples:* Denver, Colorado   Dover, Delaware

Write the names of the cities and states correctly. Use capital letters and commas where they are needed.

1. akron ohio   _____

2. hilo hawaii   _____

3. macon georgia   _____

4. nome alaska   _____

5. provo utah   _____

Rewrite the sentences. Use capital letters and commas where they are needed.

6. Nancy lives in barnet vermont.

_____

7. Mr. Hill went to houston texas.

_____

8. Did Bruce like bend oregon?

_____

9. Will Amy visit newark ohio?

_____

Using Commas in Dates

Put a comma between the day of the month and the year.

Examples: March 2, 1836
January 1, 2014

Write these dates correctly. Use capital letters, periods, and commas where they are needed.

1. dec 12 1948 _____

2. mar 27 1965 _____

3. sept 8 1994 _____

4. nov 1 2000 _____

5. jan 5 1995 _____

Complete the sentences. Write the date correctly on the line.

6. Jim was born on _____.
(august 10 1967)

7. Jen's birthday is _____.
(Oct 17 1983)

8. Maria visited on _____. (february 8 2013)

9. Dad's party was on _____. (july 29 2008)

10. Carrie started school on _____. (sept 3 2010)

11. Luis lost his first tooth on _____. (oct 20 2012)

12. I was born on _____.

Unit 4: Vocabulary and Usage
Rhyming Words

Words that end with the same sounds are **rhyming words**.

Examples: car—star   boat—goat

A **rhyme** is two or more lines that end with rhyming words. Many rhymes are silly or funny.

Example: The cat took a rocket trip to the <u>moon</u>.
              It left in July and came back in <u>June</u>.

How to Write a Rhyme

1. Write two lines.

2. End each line with a rhyming word.

Choose a word from the box to finish each rhyme.

cow	dog	bee	hat

1. Did you ever see a cat

wear a funny _____?

2. The cat climbed up a tree

and sang a song with a _____.

3. The bee said, "Meow,"

and flew away to visit the _____.

4. The cow watched a frog

hop over a _____.

Using Formal and Informal English

You use **informal English** when you talk or write to friends.

Examples:

Hey Bobby!   Are you gonna come over?

You use **formal English** in school and when you speak or write to adults.

Examples:

Hello, Mr. Wagner.   Do you plan to visit?

Write formal or informal to describe the writing.

1. Oh, no. I goofed up!

_____

2. Male brown bears can weigh 800 pounds. They can live for up to 25 years in the wild.

_____

3. Hey Tom! Wanna play basketball later?

_____

Read each example. Would you use formal or informal English? Write formal or informal to describe the writing.

4. a school report about the moon

_____

5. a note to the school principal

_____

Synonyms

Words that mean almost the same thing are called **synonyms**.

Examples: Grin is a synonym of smile.
Sleep is a synonym of rest.

Read each sentence. Find a synonym in the box for each underlined word. Write it on the line.

dog	dad	gift	large	great	home
road	sad	sick	sleep	small	yell

1. I walked across the street. _____

2. I went into my house. _____

3. I was so unhappy. _____

4. I almost felt ill. _____

5. It was my birthday. No one gave me a present. _____

6. Then, I saw something little. _____

7. It had big eyes. _____

8. It was a little puppy. _____

9. I began to shout. _____

10. "What a wonderful present!" _____

11. My father did remember my birthday. _____

12. I don't think I will rest tonight. _____

Antonyms

> Words that mean the opposite are called **antonyms**.
>
> *Examples:*   <u>Up</u> is an antonym of <u>down</u>.
> <u>Day</u> is an antonym of <u>night</u>.

Draw a line to the antonym for each underlined word.

1. a <u>hard</u> bed   dark

2. a <u>short</u> story   happy

3. a <u>light</u> color   long

4. <u>off</u> the table   low

5. a <u>sad</u> movie   on

6. a <u>high</u> bridge   soft

Write the antonym for the underlined word.

7. When you are not <u>wet</u>, you are _____.
   (happy, dry)

8. I like to run <u>fast</u>, not _____.
   (slow, far)

9. When food isn't <u>good</u>, it tastes _____.
   (hot, bad)

10. Summer is <u>hot</u>, and winter is _____.
    (cold, snow)

11. A traffic light turns red for <u>stop</u> and green for _____.
    (high, go)

12. Some questions are <u>easy</u>. Others are _____.
    (not, hard)

Homographs

Homographs are words that are spelled alike but have different meanings. Some homographs are pronounced differently.

Examples:

<u>felt</u>: a soft kind of cloth   <u>wind</u>: moving air

<u>felt</u>: sensed on the skin   <u>wind</u>: to turn a knob

---

Look at each pair of pictures. Read each sentence. Then, write the letter of the correct meaning on the line.

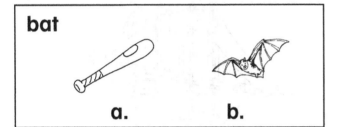

bat

     a.   b.

____ **1.** Tony has a wooden bat.

____ **2.** The bat sleeps during the day.

____ **3.** The bat broke when Alberto hit the ball.

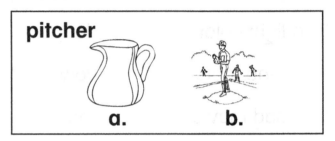

pitcher

     a.   b.

____ **7.** I put juice in the pitcher.

____ **8.** The pitcher threw the ball too low.

____ **9.** The milk pitcher was empty.

plant

     a.   b.

____ **4.** Lee will plant a tree.

____ **5.** The farmer wants to plant his crops in the fall.

____ **6.** Jody grew a plant.

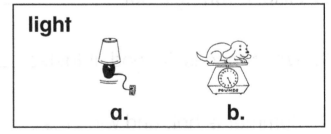

light

     a.   b.

____ **10.** I will turn on the light.

____ **11.** The puppy is light.

____ **12.** There is only one light in my room.

Homophones

> **Homophones** are words that sound the same but are spelled differently.
>
> Use <u>hear</u> to mean "to listen to."
>
> *Example*:   We <u>hear</u> the bell ringing.
>
> Use <u>here</u> to mean "to this place" or "at this place."
>
> *Example*:   Bring the ticket <u>here</u>.
>
> Use <u>your</u> when you mean "belonging to you."
>
> *Example*:   Do you have <u>your</u> homework?
>
> Use <u>you're</u> when you mean "you are."
>
> *Example*:   <u>You're</u> in trouble now.

Write <u>hear</u> or <u>here</u> to complete each sentence correctly.

1. Did you _____ that the circus is coming?

2. Is it coming _____ soon?

3. Yes, it will be _____ today.

4. I think I _____ the music now.

Write <u>your</u> or <u>you're</u> to complete each sentence correctly.

5. _____ a good skater, Eric.

6. Pull _____ laces tight.

7. Now, _____ ready to skate safely.

More Homophones

Homophones are words that sound the same but are spelled differently.

Use <u>write</u> to mean "to put words on paper."

Example: Ben likes to <u>write</u> at his desk.

Use <u>right</u> to mean "correct."

Example: Your answer is <u>right</u>.

Use <u>right</u> to mean "the opposite of left."

Example: Turn <u>right</u> to get to my school.

Write <u>right</u> or <u>write</u> to complete each sentence correctly.

1. Chris will _____ on the board.

2. Everything was _____ on Martha's math paper.

3. We turn _____ to go to the lunchroom.

4. Our class is learning to _____ stories.

5. Kim drew the picture on the _____ side.

6. Luis can _____ in Spanish.

7. The teacher marked the _____ answers.

8. Be sure you do the _____ page.

9. Jenna will _____ about her birthday party.

10. James colors with his _____ hand.

Troublesome Words

Use <u>two</u> to mean "the number 2."

Example: <u>Two</u> children worked together.

Use <u>too</u> to mean "more than enough."

Example: There are <u>too</u> many people on the bus.

Use <u>too</u> to mean "also."

Example: May I help, <u>too</u>?

Use <u>to</u> to mean "toward" or "to do something."

Example: Let's go <u>to</u> the library <u>to</u> find Kim.

Write <u>two</u>, <u>too</u>, or <u>to</u> to complete each sentence.

1. The children were working _____ make a class library.

2. Andy had _____ books in his hand.

3. He gave them _____ Ms. Diaz.

4. Ms. Diaz was happy _____ get the books.

5. "We can never have _____ many books," she said.

6. Rosa said she would bring _____ or three books.

7. James wanted to bring some, _____.

8. Joann found a book that was _____ old.

9. Pages started _____ fall out when she picked it up.

10. Soon, everyone would have new books _____ read.

11. We can take out _____ of these books at a time.

More Troublesome Words

Use <u>there</u> when you mean "in that place."

Example: The dinosaur is over <u>there</u>.

Use <u>their</u> when you mean "belonging to them."

Example: This is <u>their</u> swamp.

<u>They're</u> is a contraction for <u>they are</u>. Use <u>they're</u> when you mean "they are."

Example: <u>They're</u> eating leaves from the trees.

Circle the correct word in ( ) to complete each sentence.

1. Is this (their, they're) food?

2. (There, They're) huge animals.

3. A big one is over (there, their).

4. Once, it was (there, their) land.

5. Dinosaurs lived (they're, there) for a while.

6. (They're, There) everywhere!

7. (They're, There) the two biggest dinosaurs.

8. The faster dinosaur is resting (their, there).

9. Small dinosaurs lived (they're, there) long ago.

10. (Their, There) land was different then.

11. I see some more dinosaurs over (they're, there).

12. (They're, There) in the lake.

Compound Words

> Sometimes two words can be put together to make a new word. The new word is called a **compound word**.
>
> *Examples:*
>
> lunch + room = lunchroom   every + day = everyday
>
> You can also look at parts of a compound word to figure out its meaning.
>
> *Examples:*   bookshelf = a shelf for books
> spaceship = a ship that goes to space

Write compound words. Pick words from Box 1 and Box 2. Write the new word in Box 3.

	Box 1	Box 2	Box 3
1.	sun	noon	_____
2.	after	glasses	_____
3.	play	ground	_____
4.	birth	book	_____
5.	scrap	day	_____

Write a compound word to finish each sentence. You may use the compound words you made above.

6. Dana was wearing _____ in class.

7. In the _____, Dana was sent to the principal's office.

8. Brad put a picture of the school in his _____.

Root Words

The **root** of a word is the main part. Word parts can be added to the beginning and end of a root word to make new words. You can look for a root word to help you find the meaning of a word.

Examples:	**root word**	**+**	**word part**	**=**	**new word**
	add	+	ition	=	<u>add</u>ition
	color	+	ful	=	<u>color</u>ful
	word part	**+**	**root word**	**=**	**new word**
	un	+	lock	=	un<u>lock</u>
	re	+	play	=	re<u>play</u>

Write the root of each word.

1. weekly   _____

2. unhelpful   _____

3. dislike   _____

4. kindness   _____

5. preheat   _____

Look at each word in bold print. Write the root word to tell the word's meaning.

6. **Players** are people who _____ a game.

7. When you do **addition**, you _____ numbers together.

8. **Sadness** is a time when you feel _____.

9. A **duckling** is a baby _____.

10. When you **rewrite** something, you _____ it again.

Prefixes

A **prefix** is a group of letters added to the beginning of a word. Adding a prefix to a word changes its meaning.

Examples: The old woman was <u>happy</u>.
The old woman was <u>unhappy</u>.

Prefix	Meaning	Example
un	not	<u>un</u>clear
re	again	<u>re</u>write

Read each sentence. Underline the word that has a prefix. Tell the meaning of the word.

1. The old man was unable to find something to wear.

   _____

2. The old woman reopened the drawer.

   _____

3. She told the old man they were unlucky.

   _____

4. The old man felt this was unfair.

   _____

5. He was very unhappy.

6. The woman asked the man to rewind the yarn.

   _____

7. The old woman rewashed the socks.

   _____

8. Could the socks be uneven?

   _____

9. The old man refilled his wife's glass.

   _____

10. The farmer's wife reknitted the sweater.

    _____

Suffixes

A **suffix** is a group of letters added to the end of a word. Adding a suffix to a word changes its meaning.

Examples:
Josef's parents were <u>helpless</u>.
The doctor was <u>helpful</u>.

Suffix	Meaning	Example
ful	full of	hope<u>ful</u>
less	without	use<u>less</u>
able	able to be	break<u>able</u>

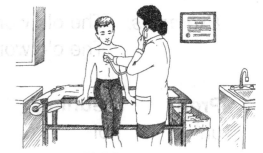

Read each sentence. Underline the word that has a suffix. Tell the meaning of the word.

1. Is Josef careful? _____

2. Josef thought the game was harmless. _____

Complete each sentence with a word from the box. Tell the meaning of the word you chose.

hopeful   dreadful   thankful

3. Josef's parents had a _____ shock!

_____

4. They were _____ the chair would not break.

_____

5. When Josef came out of the hospital, he was very _____.

_____

Using Context Clues

> **Context clues** are the clues that help you figure out the meaning of a word you may not know.
>
> *Example:*　During the <u>blizzard</u>, there was strong wind and heavy snow.
>
> What does the word <u>blizzard</u> mean? Look for clues.
>
> The words *strong wind* and *heavy snow* are context clues. A <u>blizzard</u> is a big snowstorm.

Circle the clues that help you understand the meaning of the underlined word. Then, write the meaning on the line.

1. We came home from the store and put our <u>groceries</u> on the shelves.

   _____

2. The <u>tornado</u> had strong winds that swirled and tossed cars through the air.

   _____

3. Brian <u>swiftly</u> raced around the track and passed the other runners.

   _____

4. Jim liked to play in the tall grasses and wide open spaces of the <u>prairie</u>.

   _____

5. The <u>woodpecker</u> grabbed a cherry in her beak and flew away.

   _____

Word Choices

Word choices help paint a clear picture in a reader's mind.

Word choices can make something sound good or bad.

Examples:

The bird <u>chirped</u>. = The sound was cheerful. (good)

The bird <u>squawked</u>. = The sound was loud. (not good)

Word choices can also be used to show an exact meaning in a sentence.

Examples:

I <u>stared</u> at the clock. = I looked at the clock for a while.

I <u>glanced</u> at the clock. = I looked quickly at the clock.

Circle the word in ( ) that best matches the meaning of each sentence.

1. I bit into the (hard, crisp) apple. It was so good!

2. My dog Fifi really wanted to chase the squirrel. She (tugged, yanked) on her leash.

3. I didn't want my balloon to float away. I tied a (string, thread) around it.

4. Grandpa made a swing for us in the yard. He used (rope, string) to hang it from the tree.

5. I was late for the school bus. I (rushed, walked) out the door.

6. I slept well in the (mushy, soft) bed at Aunt Marge's house.

7. The (wind, breeze) knocked over a big tree in the park.

8. Kwan was (glad, thrilled) when he won the prize.

9. The horse (hopped, leaped) over the fence.

Unit 5: Writing
Writing Sentences

> Remember that sentences have a naming part and an action part.
>
> **Naming Part**   **Action Part**
> Sara   won the race.

Draw a line from a naming part to an action part to make sentences.

Naming Part	**Action Part**
1. Grandma	baked.
2. Aunt Sue	sings.
3. My friend	skates.
4. Earl's dad	reads.
5. Kiko's mom	cooks.
6. Jon's sister	played.

Write sentences with the naming parts and action parts you put together. Add some describing words of your own.

7. _____

8. _____

9. _____

10. _____

11. _____

12. _____

Paragraphs

A **paragraph** is a group of sentences that tells about one main idea. The first line of a paragraph is indented. This means the first word is moved in a little from the left side.

The first sentence in a paragraph often tells the main idea. The other sentences tell about the main idea.

Example:

A safe home keeps people from getting hurt. Shoes or toys should not be left on the stairs. Matches, medicines, and cleaners should be locked safely away.

How to Write a Paragraph

1. Write a sentence that tells the main idea.

2. Indent the first line.

3. Write sentences that tell more about the main idea.

Write three sentences that tell about this main idea.

There are many things you can do to be safe at school.

_____

_____

_____

_____

_____

Main Idea

> The **main idea** of a paragraph is often in the first sentence. It tells what the paragraph is about.
>
> *Example:*
> **I have nice neighbors**. Ms. Hill gives me flowers. Mr. Stone always smiles and waves. Miss Higgins plays ball with me.

Read each paragraph. Write the sentence that tells the main idea.

Uncle Joe is a funny man. He tells jokes about elephants. He does magic tricks that don't work. He makes funny faces when he tells stories. He wears funny hats. He always makes me laugh.

1. _____

_____

Dad told us a funny story about his dog. When Dad was a little boy, he had a dog named Tiger. One day, Dad forgot his lunch. Dad said Tiger would bring it to school. A friend thought it would be a real tiger.

2. _____

_____

Firefighters are brave people. They go into burning buildings. They put out fires. They teach families how to be safe in their homes.

3. _____

_____

Supporting Details

> The other sentences in a paragraph give **details** about the main idea in the beginning sentence.
>
> *Example:*
>
> I have nice neighbors. **Ms. Hill gives me flowers. Mr. Stone always smiles and waves. Miss Higgins plays ball with me.**

Read each paragraph. Circle the main idea. Underline the sentences that give details about the main idea.

1. Uncle Joe is a funny man. He tells jokes about elephants. He does magic tricks that don't work. He makes funny faces when he tells stories. He wears funny hats. He always makes me laugh.

2. Dad told us a funny story about his dog. When Dad was a little boy, he had a dog named Tiger. One day Dad forgot his lunch. Dad said Tiger would bring it to school. A friend thought it would be a real tiger.

3. Firefighters are brave people. They go into burning buildings. They put out fires. They teach families how to be safe in their homes.

Order in Paragraphs

The sentences in a paragraph tell things in the order in which they happened.

Words such as <u>first</u>, <u>second</u>, <u>third</u>, <u>next</u>, <u>then</u>, and <u>last</u> can help tell when things happened.

Example:

Jane got ready for bed. **First**, she took a bath. **Next**, she brushed her teeth. **Then**, she put on her pajamas. **Last**, she read a story and got into bed.

Write *1, 2, 3,* or *4* to show what happened first, second, third, and last.

Eva planted flowers. First, she got a shovel. Next, she dug some holes in the garden. Then, she put the flowers into the holes. Last, she put the shovel back in its place.

_____ Then, she put the flowers into the holes.

_____ Next, she dug some holes in the garden.

_____ Last, she put the shovel back in its place.

_____ First, she got a shovel.

Dan and Larry washed the car. First, they got the car wet. Next, they put soap all over it. Then, they washed all the soap off. Last, they dried the car.

_____ They put soap all over the car.

_____ They washed all the soap off.

_____ Dan and Larry dried the car.

_____ Dan and Larry got the car wet.

Name _____ Date _____

Personal Narrative

A **personal narrative** is a story about the writer. In a story, a writer tells about one main idea. Every story has a beginning, a middle, and an ending. A personal story has details that tell about actions, thoughts, and feelings.

Example:

One day Grandpa had a surprise for me. He took me to the zoo. First, we looked at tigers. Next, we watched playful monkeys. Then, we saw big black bears. Last, Grandpa helped me feed the seals. My day with Grandpa was wonderful!

How to Write a Paragraph About Yourself

1. Write a sentence that tells about something that happened to you. Tell where the story took place.

2. Write sentences that tell about what happened in order. Use the words <u>first</u>, <u>next</u>, <u>then</u>, and <u>last</u>.

3. Use details to tell what you did, what you saw, and how you felt.

Read the *Example* paragraph above. Answer the questions.

1. Where does the story take place?

   _____

2. What happens after they look at the tigers?

   _____

3. What happens last?

   _____

Name _____ Date _____

Personal Narrative, part 2

Finish the paragraph. Add words that tell about yourself.

I had a good day at school. First, I _____

_____. Next, I _____.

Then, I ate lunch with my friend _____.

Last, I _____

_____.

How to Revise and Edit

1. Read your story carefully. Does it have a beginning, middle, and end?

2. Look for mistakes. Are words spelled correctly? Does each sentence begin with a capital letter? Does each sentence end with an end mark?

3. Look for places to add details. How did something look? How did you feel?

Trade the story you wrote above with a partner. Tell your partner about mistakes and about details that can be added. Then, use your partner's ideas to improve your story. Write it on the lines below.

_____

_____

_____

_____

Personal Narrative, part 3

Finish the chart. Use the chart to write a new story about yourself.

Beginning	Middle	Ending
Who is in the story? Where does the story happen?	What happens?	How do things work out?

Trade stories with a partner. Tell your partner ways to make the story better. Then, use your partner's ideas to revise and edit your story. Write your story on the lines below.

_____

_____

_____

_____

_____

_____

_____

_____

_____

_____

_____

Describing Paragraph

In a paragraph that **describes**, a writer tells about a person, place, or thing. The sentences have describing words that help the reader see, hear, taste, smell, and feel.

Example:

Many birds visit my backyard. Red cardinals make nests in our bushes. Many tiny hummingbirds buzz around the yellow flowers in our garden. Robins chirp sweetly and wake me in the morning.

How to Write a Paragraph That Describes

1. Write a sentence that tells whom or what the paragraph is about.

2. Write sentences that tell more about the main idea.

3. Use describing words in your sentences.

Read the *Example* describing paragraph. Answer the questions.

1. What is the topic of the paragraph?

_____

2. Which words tell what the birds are like?

_____

3. Write a describing sentence to add to the paragraph.

_____

Describing Paragraph, part 2

Finish the paragraph. Add describing words.

The little woman put on her _____ hat.

She went outside. It was a _____ day. The

sky was _____. The little woman felt

_____.

Finish the chart. Write describing words about your topic. Use the chart to write a describing paragraph.

| My topic: _____ | | | | |

Looks	Feels	Tastes	Smells	Sounds
_____	_____	_____	_____	_____
_____	_____	_____	_____	_____
_____	_____	_____	_____	_____

_____

_____

_____

_____

_____

Friendly Letter

A **friendly letter** is a letter you write to someone you know. It has five parts. They are the date, greeting, body, closing, and signature.

Example:

date —| October 22, 2003

greeting —| Dear Grandma,

body —| The sweater you knitted for my birthday is great! The fall days here have been chilly. It's nice to have a new, warm sweater to wear. Thank you!

closing —| Love,

signature —| Emily

How to Write a Friendly Letter

1. Choose a friend or a relative to write to.

2. Write about things you have done.

3. Be sure your letter has a date, greeting, body, closing, and signature.

4. Use capital letters and commas correctly.

Read the *Example* friendly letter. Answer the questions.

1. Whom did Emily write the letter to?

_____

2. Why did Emily write the letter?

_____

Name _____ Date _____

Friendly Letter, part 2

Think of someone you want to write to. Use the organizer below to write your friendly letter.

date _____

greeting _____

body _____

_____

_____

_____

_____

_____

_____

_____

_____

closing _____

signature _____

How-To Paragraph

In a **how-to paragraph**, a writer tells how to make or do something. The writer tells what the paragraph is about. The steps are told in order. The writer includes an ending sentence.

Example:

A bird feeder is easy to make. You will need a pine cone, string, peanut butter, and birdseed. First, tie the string to the top of the pine cone. Next, roll the pine cone in peanut butter. Then, roll it in birdseed. Last, go outside and tie the pine cone to a tree branch. Now, the birds have a tasty snack!

How to Write a How-To Paragraph

1. Write a sentence that tells what the paragraph is about.

2. Write a sentence that lists things you need.

3. Use the words <u>first</u>, <u>next</u>, <u>then</u>, and <u>last</u> to tell the steps.

4. Write an ending sentence for your paragraph.

Read the *Example* how-to paragraph. Answer the questions.

1. What does the paragraph tell how to do?

_____

2. What materials are needed?

_____

3. What does the ending sentence tell about?

_____

How-To Paragraph, part 2

Put these sentences for a how-to paragraph in order. Write *1, 2, 3, 4,* or *5* to show the order of the steps.

_____ Next, fill the can with water.   _____ Here is how to water a plant.

_____ Last, water the plant.   _____ First, get a watering can.

_____ Now, your plant will have the
water it needs.

Finish the chart. Use the chart to write a how-to paragraph.

My topic: _____
Materials needed: _____   _____   _____
Steps: 1. _____   2. _____   3. _____   4. _____

_____

_____

_____

_____

Informative Paragraph

In an **informative paragraph**, a writer gives facts and details about one topic.

Example:

Many African American people celebrate a holiday called Kwanzaa. Kwanzaa is a celebration of the customs and history of African American people. It is a gathering time for families, like Thanksgiving. The holiday is celebrated for seven days. It begins the day after Christmas. On each night of Kwanzaa, a candle is lit. Each candle stands for a rule to help people live their lives. Kwanzaa helps people learn about African American culture.

How to Write an Informative Paragraph

1. Write a sentence that tells whom or what your paragraph is about.

2. Write detail sentences. Give interesting facts about the person, animal, place, or thing.

3. Write an ending sentence.

Read the *Example* informative paragraph. Answer the questions.

1. Which sentence tells what the informative paragraph is about?

_____

2. Write one detail sentence from the paragraph.

_____

Name _____ Date _____

Informative Paragraph, part 2

Think about a topic you would like to write about. Complete the chart. You may want to use books or the Internet to find information about your topic.

Topic: _____

Main idea:

Detail 1:

Detail 2:

Detail 3:

Ending idea: _____
_____

Informative Paragraph, part 3

Use the chart from page 102 to write your informative paragraph.

_____

_____

_____

_____

_____

Read your paragraph. Look for ways to make it better. Use this checklist:

✓ Do you have a sentence that tells what your paragraph is about?

✓ Did you include at least three details?

✓ Do you have an ending sentence?

✓ Did you use correct spelling, capital letters, and punctuation?

_____

_____

_____

_____

_____

Book Report

A **book report** tells about a book and what you think about it.

Example:

The Koala by Anita Best is a good book. It has many colorful pictures and tells many facts about koalas. For example, I learned that koalas live in Australia. They live in trees and eat leaves. If you want to learn about these animals, read this book.

How to Write a Book Report

1. Write the title of the book and the author's name.

2. Tell what you think about the book. Give reasons why you feel that way.

3. Tell some facts about the book. Tell about important people, places, and things in the book.

4. Write an ending sentence to retell what you think.

Read the *Example* book report. Answer the questions.

1. What is the title of the book?

_____

2. Who wrote the book?

_____

3. What did the writer of the report think about the book?

_____

Name _____ Date _____

Book Report, part 2

Think of a book you would like to tell about. Fill in the information.

Title and author of book: _____

What I think about this book: _____

_____

Reasons I feel this way: _____

_____

Facts and details about this book: _____

_____

Ending sentence about this book: _____

_____

Use the information to write a book report. With the help of a teacher or adult, type your book report on a computer. You can print out your book report or publish it on the Internet to share with others.

_____

_____

_____

_____

_____

_____

Opinion Paragraph

An **opinion paragraph** tries to make the reader agree with the writer's opinion.

Example:
    I think that a lizard should be our class pet. A lizard is small and easy to care for. Lizards are interesting to watch, too. We could also study the lizard to learn about reptiles. Vote for the lizard!

How to Write an Opinion Paragraph

1. Write about something you feel strongly about.

2. Tell your opinion in the first sentence.

3. Give reasons why other people should feel the same way.

4. Use linking words like <u>because</u> and <u>also</u> to support your ideas.

5. Ask your reader to do something in the last sentence.

Read the *Example* opinion paragraph. Answer the questions.

1. What is the writer's opinion in the first sentence?

_____

2. What is one reason the writer gives to make the reader agree?

_____

3. What does the writer want the reader to do?

_____

Name _____ Date _____

Opinion Paragraph, part 2

Finish this opinion paragraph about a game or a toy that you really like. Try to convince a friend to get the game. Give reasons why.

You should get a _____ because

_____. This is a great game/toy because

_____.

Another thing I like about it is _____. I also

like _____. These are some reasons I love

_____. I think you will love it, too!

Read your opinion paragraph. Look for ways to make it better. Add reasons your friend should get the game or toy. Use linking words like <u>because</u> and <u>also</u> to explain your ideas. Rewrite your paragraph below.

_____

_____

_____

_____

_____

_____

_____

Opinion Paragraph, part 3

Think of something you feel strongly about. Fill in the information at the top and use it to write an opinion paragraph.

Opinion: _____

Reason 1: _____

_____

Reason 2: _____

Reason 3 (your strongest reason): _____

_____

What the reader should do: _____

_____

_____

_____

_____

_____

_____

_____

_____

_____

Unit 6: Research Skills
Words in ABC Order

The order of letters from <u>A</u> to <u>Z</u> is called **ABC order**, or **alphabetical order**.

When words begin with the same letter, the next letter of the word is used to put the words in ABC order: <u>ca</u>pe, <u>ch</u>apel, <u>ci</u>ty.

Number the words in ABC order. Then, write the words in the correct order.

1. _____ bat
   _____ air
   _____ cat

2. _____ top
   _____ sea
   _____ rock

3. _____ egg
   _____ fish
   _____ dog

4. _____ hat
   _____ ice
   _____ gate

5. _____ joke
   _____ lake
   _____ king

6. _____ neck
   _____ owl
   _____ mail

7. _____ yes
   _____ zoo
   _____ walk

8. _____ pan
   _____ oak
   _____ nail

Name _____ Date _____

Using a Dictionary

A **dictionary** is a book that lists words and their meanings. Dictionaries also tell you how to say a word. You can use a dictionary to check the correct spelling of a word. The words in a dictionary are listed in ABC order.

Many words on a dictionary page begin with the same letter. When words begin with the same letter, the second letter is used to put the words in ABC order.

<u>se</u>eds

<u>st</u>ory

<u>su</u>n

You can use an **online dictionary** on the Internet. You type the word to see its meaning and the way to say it.

Some books have a **glossary** at the back. The glossary tells the meaning of words in the book. A glossary also uses ABC order.

Put each group of words in ABC order. Remember to use the second letter in each word if the first letter is the same.

1. noise _____

   music _____

   poem _____

2. sun _____

   rain _____

   plant _____

3. garden _____

   ground _____

   frog _____

4. afraid _____

   asleep _____

   alone _____

Name _____ Date _____

Using a Dictionary, part 2

Each word listed in the dictionary is called an **entry word**.

The two words at the top of a dictionary page are called **guide words**. The word on the left is the first entry word on the page. The word on the right is the last entry word on the page. All the other entry words on the page are in ABC order between the first and the last words.

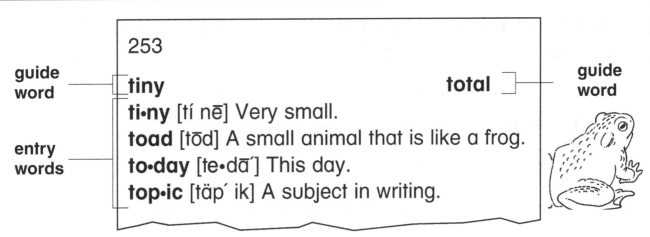

253

guide word — tiny   total — guide word

entry words —
ti•ny [tí nē] Very small.
toad [tōd] A small animal that is like a frog.
to•day [te•dā´] This day.
top•ic [täp´ ik] A subject in writing.

Use the *Example* dictionary page. Answer these questions.

1. What is the first entry word on page 253? _____

2. Would you find the word <u>think</u> on this page? _____

3. Kara wrote the word <u>tode</u> to tell about a small animal like a frog. Did

she spell the word correctly? _____

4. What entry word means "very small"? _____

5. Could the entry word <u>together</u> be on this page? _____

Why or why not? _____

6. Ed wrote the word <u>toppic</u> in a report. What is the correct spelling?

_____

Using a Dictionary, part 3

> Some entry words have more than one meaning. Each meaning has a number. Each meaning is followed by example sentences that show how to use the entry word.

bump [bump] **1** To knock against: We <u>bumped</u> heads. **2** A part that sticks out: The car rolled over a <u>bump</u> in the road.

burst [burst] **1** To break apart suddenly: The balloon <u>burst</u>. **2** To give way to a strong feeling: Grandfather and I <u>burst</u> into laughter.

Read the dictionary entries. Answer the questions.

1. What word can mean "to break apart"? _____

2. What is the example sentence for meaning 2 of <u>burst</u>?

_____

3. Which word can mean "to knock against"? _____

Look at the online dictionary entry. Answer the questions.

lit·ter ◀ **1** Trash that is left on the ground: There was <u>litter</u> in the street after the parade. **2** A group of baby animals: The cat had a <u>litter</u> of five kittens.

4. What is meaning 1 of <u>litter</u>?

_____

5. Write your own example sentence for meaning 2 of <u>litter</u>.

_____

Using a Dictionary, part 4

Use these words from the glossary of a book to answer the questions. Write <u>yes</u> or <u>no</u>.

always	at all times
animal	a living thing that is not a plant
bed	a place to sleep
dark	without light
green	the color of grass
hay	grass cut, dried, and used as food for cows and horses
hungry	needing food
kitten	a young cat
ladder	a set of steps used to climb up and down
library	a building where books are kept

1. Is <u>hay</u> something that alligators eat? _____

2. Is a <u>bed</u> a place for swimming? _____

3. Is grass <u>green</u>? _____

4. Is a flower an <u>animal</u>? _____

5. Can you use a <u>ladder</u> to climb to the roof? _____

6. Is a baby pig called a <u>kitten</u>? _____

7. Is a <u>library</u> a place for food? _____

8. Are you <u>hungry</u> after having lunch? _____

Name _____ Date _____

Using an Encyclopedia

An **encyclopedia** is a set of books that has facts on many subjects. Each book in a set is called a volume. The volumes list subjects in ABC order. You can also use a computer to find online encyclopedias. To find information in an online encyclopedia, you type the name of the topic.

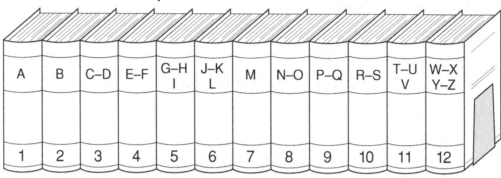

A	B	C–D	E–F	G–H I	J–K L	M	N–O	P–Q	R–S	T–U V	W–X Y–Z
1	2	3	4	5	6	7	8	9	10	11	12

Use the model encyclopedia in the picture. Write the number of the volume in which you would find each of these subjects.

1. Ohio River _____

2. explorers _____

3. Rocky Mountains _____

4. cows _____

5. United States _____

6. farming _____

Write the word or words you would use to look up the following subjects in an encyclopedia.

7. pretty butterflies   _____

8. kinds of dogs   _____

9. trees in the United States   _____

10. Florida history   _____

Name _____ Date _____

Parts of a Book

The **title page** tells the title of a book. It gives the name of the author. The author is the person who wrote the book.

The **table of contents** lists the chapters or parts of the book. It tells the page where each chapter or part begins.

Some books have an **index**. It is in ABC order. It tells the pages where things can be found.

Title Page	Table of Contents	Index
	Contents	Apartments, 2, 7
Kinds of Houses	1. Brick Houses.......1	Basements, 25
by Jack Builder	2. City Houses 5	Ceilings, 2, 9
	3. Country Houses..8	Concrete, 4, 16
	4. Wood Houses ... 15	Doors, 12, 17

Look at the sample pages. Answer these questions.

1. What is the title of the book? _____

2. Who wrote the book? _____

3. How many chapters are in this book? _____

4. On what page does chapter 4 begin? _____

5. On which pages can you find facts about ceilings? _____

Parts of a Book, part 2

The **title page** is in the front of a book. It tells you the title of the book. It tells you who wrote the book. It tells you who drew the pictures (illustrated) the book. And it tells you what company published the book.

Look at this title page from a book about cats. Then, write your answers to the questions below on the lines.

ALL ABOUT CATS

by
Patricia L. Keller

Illustrated by
Richard H. Green

Coaster Press
New York

1. What is the title of the book? _____

2. Who wrote the book? _____

3. Who illustrated the book? _____

4. What company published the book? _____

Parts of a Book, part 3

The **table of contents** is near the front of a book. It tells you what each chapter of the book is about. When you want to know what a book is about, you should read the table of contents.

Look at this page from the book All About Cats. Then, write the correct answers to the questions on the lines below.

Table of Contents

CHAPTER	PAGE
1 Kinds of Cats	3
2 Picking the Right Cat	7
3 Taking Care of Your Cat	12
4 Playing with Your Cat	18
5 If Your Cat Gets Sick	23
6 Cats in the Wild	27

1. What chapter tells you what to do if your cat gets sick? _____

2. What chapter tells you about different kinds of cats? _____

3. What page tells you how to pick the right cat? _____

4. What is the name of the chapter on page 27?

_____

Name _____ Date _____

Kinds of Books

Some books are called **fiction**. They are stories about make-believe people and things. Here are some titles of books that are fiction.

Ask Mr. Bear

The Bears Go to the Hospital

Nonfiction books tell about real people or things. These books are nonfiction.

The Hospital Book

Who Keeps Us Safe?

A library has fiction and nonfiction books. The fiction books are in one part of the library. The nonfiction books are in another part.

Read about each book. Tell if the book is <u>fiction</u> or <u>nonfiction</u>.

1. a book about a magic bear _____

2. a book that tells how to keep your home safe _____

3. a book that tells how to ride a bicycle safely _____

4. a book about a bear that can draw _____

5. a book about a house that can talk _____

6. a book about the fire department _____

7. a book about a dog that can fly _____

Answer Key

page 1

Order may vary. **1.** apple, **2.** bird, **3.** boy, **4.** car, **5.** chair, **6.** desk, **7.** girl, **8.** grass, **9.** pen, **10.** rug, **11.** tree, **12.** truck, **13.** girl, apple, **14.** bird, tree, **15.** chair, desk, **16.** boy, chair, **17.** girl, truck

page 2

1. sister, park, **2.** car, mother, **3.** dog, **4.** boy, birds, trees, **5.** playground, **6.** cat, slide; Chart: Person: sister, mother, boy; Place: park, playground; Thing: car, trees, slide; Animal: dog, birds, cat

page 3

Order may vary. **1.** Bob's Bikes, **2.** Bridge Road, **3.** China, **4.** Elf Corn, **5.** Gabriel, **6.** Lindsey, **7.** New York City, **8.** Oregon, **9.** Pat Green, **10.** State Street, **11.** Hill's Store, **12.** Baker Street, **13.** Stone Library, **14.** Emily Fuller

page 4

Order may vary. **1.** team, **2.** herd, **3.** bunch, **4.** group, **5.** flock, **6.** family, **7.** class, **8.** crowd, **9.** class, **10.** deck, **11.** band, **12.** bunch, **13.** herd, **14.** flock

page 5

1. Where did Jack Sprat go?, **2.** Mary saw her friend Jill., **3.** Did Mr. or Mrs. Sprat go with them?, **4.** They met Ms. Muffet along the way., **5.–6.** Proper nouns will vary.

page 6

1. They walked along Main Street., **2.** My uncle drove through Indiana and Ohio., **3.** We went on a trip to Mexico., **4.–8.** Proper nouns will vary.

page 7

1. Wednesday, **2.** February, **3.** Saturday, **4.** Thanksgiving, **5.–7.** Answers will vary.

page 8

1. boys, **2.** girl, **3.** robe, **4.** stars, **5.** moon, **6.** house, **7.** door, **8.** treats, **9.** cats, **10.** dogs, **11.** owl, **12.** stars, **13.** trees, **14.** hands

page 9

1. caps, **2.** chairs, **3.** girls, **4.** trees, **5.** flags, **6.** boys, **7.** seeds, **8.** carrots, **9.** peas, **10.** friends, **11.** gardens

page 10

1. lunches, **2.** dresses, **3.** glasses, **4.** dishes, **5.** boxes, **6.** watches, **7.** foxes, **8.** benches, **9.** inches, **10.** brushes, **11.** classes, **12.** churches

page 11

1. woman, **2.** men, **3.** child, **4.** feet, **5.** mice, **6.** mice, **7.** feet, **8.** teeth, **9.** men, **10.** fish

page 12

1. We, **2.** She or He, **3.** She or He, **4.** It, **5.** She or He, **6.** It, **7.** They, **8.** We, **9.** They, **10.** We

page 13

1. themselves, **2.** myself, **3.** ourselves, **4.** himself, **5.** myself, **6.** herself, **7.** themselves, **8.** ourselves

page 14

1. I, **2.** me, **3.** me, **4.** I, **5.** Susan and I, **6.** Tina and me, **7.** Tina and I, **8.** Susan and me

page 15

1. runs, **2.** kicks, **3.** breaks, **4.** looks, **5.** runs, **6.** talks, **7.** sends, **8.** pays; **9.–13.** Answers may vary. **9.** The boy reads., **10.** The baby cries., **11.** The rabbit hops., **12.** The birds sing., **13.** The dogs bark.

page 16

1. skips, **2.** play, **3.** hug, **4.** purrs, **5.** barks, **6.** hide, **7.** waves, **8.** blows, **9.** follows, **10.** sees, **11.** hears, **12.** move, **13.** hoots, **14.** take, **15.** eat

page 17

1. have, **2.** have, **3.** had, **4.** has, **5.** has, **6.** has, **7.** have, **8.** had, **9.** has, **10.** have, **11.** have, **12.** had

page 18

1. are, **2.** are, **3.** were, **4.** is, **5.** are, **6.** were, **7.** is, **8.** am, **9.** was, **10.** is

page 19

1. plays, **2.** runs, **3.** dance, **4.** wait, **5.** leaps; Paragraph (Answers may vary.): takes, sits, asks, dances, stands, walks

page 20

1. played, **2.** visited, **3.** looked, **4.** jumped, **5.** leaned, **6.** helped, **7.** laughed, **8.** The girls played in the park., **9.** They climbed over rocks., **10.** Their fathers called to them.

page 21

1. sat, **2.** came, **3.** went, **4.** go, **5.** hid, **6.** told, **7.** goes, went, **8.** comes, came, **9.** sit, sat, **10.** run, ran

page 22

1. played, **2.** called, **3.** wanted, **4.** laughed, **5.** jumped, **6.** played, **7.** laughing, **8.** playing, **9.** talking, **10.** Carmen helped Grandma cook yesterday., **11.** Grandma is cooking some soup today.

page 23

1. are, **2.** is, **3.** are, **4.** is, **5.** are, **6.** are, **7.** are, **8.** are, **9.–10.** Sentences will vary.

page 24

1. were, **2.** was, **3.** were, **4.** were, **5.** were, **6.** was, **7.** was, **8.** were, **9.–10.** Sentences will vary.

page 25

1. sees, **2.** saw, **3.** sees, **4.** sees, **5.** saw, **6.** saw, **7.** see, **8.** saw, **9.** saw, **10.** see, **11.** saw, **12.** sees

Answer Key
Core Skills Language Arts, Grade 2

page 26

1. ran; Horses ran wild long ago., 2. run; A horse can run ten miles every day., 3. run; Can you run as fast as a horse?, 4. ran; Mandy ran in a race last week., 5. runs; Carl runs home from school now., 6. runs; Now, Mandy runs after Carl., 7. run; How far can you run?

page 27

1. give, 2. gave, 3. gives, 4. gave, 5. gave, 6. gave, 7. gave, 8. gave, 9.–11. Sentences will vary.

page 28

1. do, 2. does, 3. does, 4. does, 5. does, 6. do, 7. does, 8. do, 9. does, 10. do, 11.–12. Sentences will vary.

page 29

1. had, 2. has, 3. have, 4. have, 5. has, 6. had, 7. has, 8. has, 9. have, 10. had, 11. had, 12. has

page 30

Answers may vary. 1. pink, 2. long, 3. brown, 4. round, 5. juicy, 6. tiny

page 31

Answers will vary. 1. tired, 2. happy, 3. many, 4. one, 5. hungry, 6. some, 7. three, 8. sleepy

page 32

2. brighter, 3. tallest, 4. fast, 5. thicker, 6. biggest, 7. wider, 8. oldest

page 33

1. an, 2. a, 3. a, 4. an, 5. a, 6. an, 7. an, 8. an, 9. a, 10. a, 11. an, 12. a, 13. an, 14. an, 15. a, 16. a, 17. a, 18. an, 19. an, 20. an, 21. a, 22. a

page 34

Answers may vary. 1. quietly, 2. outside, 3. loudly, 4. quickly, 5. inside, 6. everywhere, 7. later, 8. tomorrow

page 35

Answers may vary. 1. early, 2. today, 3. up, 4. there, 5. neatly, 6. over, 7. Soon, 8. Later, 9. down

page 36

1. slowly, 2. slow, 3. small, 4. loudly, 5. big, 6. hungry, 7. now, 8.–9. Sentences will vary.

page 37

1. sadly, 2. sad, 3. quick, 4. quiet; Paragraph (Answers may vary.): yesterday, new, carefully, colorful, blue, over, happy

page 38

1. no, 2. yes, 3. no, 4. yes, 5. yes, 6. yes, 7. no, 8. no, 9. yes, 10. yes, 11. yes, 12. no, 13. yes

page 39

Answers may vary. 1. Mrs. Brown lives on my street., 2. Our building is made of wood., 3. Four families live in our building., 4. Our class went on a picnic., 5. Jennifer was climbing the tree., 6. The sun shines all day., 7. Corn and beans grow on a farm., 8. The wagon has a broken wheel., 9. The mother goat fed the baby goat., 10. The boat sailed in strong winds., 11. The fisher caught seven fish., 12. Some of the fish were sold in the store., 13. Our team won ten games., 14. Our batters hit the ball a lot., 15. The ballpark was full of fans., 16. Sentences will vary.

page 40

Answers will vary.

page 41

1. My family and I, 2. Sami Harper, 3. Miss Jenkins, 4. Mr. Chang, 5. Henry, 6. Mr. Byrne, 7. Mrs. Lee, 8. Mr. and Mrs. Diaz, 9. Jeanine, 10. Mr. Wolf, 11. Amy Taft, 12. Mr. Dowd, 13. Mrs. Clark, 14. Carolyn and Alberto, 15. Julie

page 42

1. fly, 2. buzz, 3. barks, 4. quack, 5. hops, 6. roar, 7. moo, 8. cluck; Sentences will vary.

page 43

1. My brother eats apples., 2. Elizabeth drinks milk., 3. Kim likes peanut butter., 4. Justin wants bread., 5. Chris plants corn., 6. Chang caught a fish., 7. Dad cooks breakfast.

page 44

1. telling, 2. telling, 3. asking, 4. not a sentence, 5. telling, 6. not a sentence, 7. telling, 8. asking, 9. telling

page 45

1. statement, 2. question, 3. statement, 4. question, 5. statement, 6. question, 7. exclamation, 8. statement, 9. question, 10. exclamation

page 46

Sentences will vary. Be sure each sentence is the specified kind.

page 47

1. John gave seeds to Sara and told her to plant them., 2. Sara planted the seeds and looked at the ground., 3. Sara sang songs to her seeds and read stories to them., 4. The rain fell on the seeds and helped them grow.

page 48

1. The farmer and his family stood in the doorway., 2. The hunter and the bear stayed with the family., 3. The mice and the children ran out the door., 4. The hunter and the bear went home.

page 49

1. Vince has a ball, and I have a bat., 2. Mom drives a car, and Dad drives a truck., 3. Jim has a dog, and Amy has a cat., 4. Mr. Lopez teaches art, and Mrs. Moore teaches science.

page 50

1. brown, large, 2. hungry, berries, fish, 3. turned over, the bear, 4. sleeping, the loud noise

page 51

Answers will vary. Be sure each new sentence contains describing words.

page 52

1. The ant climbed down a blade of grass. He (or She) fell into the spring., 2. The bird pulled off a leaf. He (or She) let the leaf fall into the water., 3. The hunter saw a lion. He spread his net., 4. The lion and I live in the woods. We are friends.

page 53

Answers will vary. Possible responses: 1. stroll, 2. race, 3. pedal, 4. speed, 5. zooms, 6. jogs, 7. skip, 8. travels, 9. sails

page 54

1. Eric Carle, 2. Beverly Cleary, 3. Diane Dillon, 4. Alicia Acker, 5. Ezra Jack Keats; 6.–8. The first letter of these words should be circled: 6. mother, grandma, 7. grandma, grandpa, 8. uncle carlos, aunt kathy, 9. Mario Martinez told me a story., 10. Ichiro and I played ball.

page 55

1. C.D., 2. C.A.C., 3. M.B., 4. M.T., 5. K.S., 6. T.L.T., 7. I.B., 8. C.L.W., 9. J.W.A., 10. L.B. Hopkins, 11. A. Martinez, 12. Patricia A. Rosen, 13. The box was for M.S. Mills., 14. D.E. Ellis sent it to her.

page 56

1. Mrs. Ruth Scott, 2. Mr. Kurt Wiese, 3. Miss E. Garcia, 4. Ms. Carol Baylor, 5. Mr. and Mrs. H. Cox, 6. Dr. S. Tomas Rios, 7. Mrs. H. Stone is here to see Dr. Brooks., 8. Mr. F. Green and Ms. Miller are not here.

page 57

1. James lives in Dayton, Ohio., 2. His house is on Market St., 3. I think Thomas Park is in this town., 4. We went to Mathis Lake for a picnic., 5. Is Main Street far away?

page 58

1. Monday, 2. Friday, 3. February, 4. Answers will vary., 5. November, 6. Tues., 7. Thurs., 8. Dec., 9. Sat., 10. Jan., 11. Sept.

page 59

1. New Year's Day, 2. Mother's Day, 3. Independence Day, 4. Labor Day, 5. Presidents' Day, 6. Thanksgiving Day, 7. Veterans Day, 8. Valentine's Day is in February., 9. Boxing Day is a British holiday., 10. Father's Day is in June.

page 60

1. Pepsi, 2. Lucky Charms, 3. Cheerios, 4. Ford Focus, 5. Xbox, 6. Barbie, 7. Tonya wears Nike tennis shoes., 8. Do you like Coke or Pepsi better?

page 61

1. Best Friends, 2. The Biggest Bear, 3. Rabbits on Roller Skates, 4. Down on the Sunny Farm; The first letter of these words should be circled: 5. we, bees, 6. the, dancing, pony, 7. my, shadow, 8. my, summer, farm

page 62

1. phone, 2. chickens, 3. train, 4. The sweet shop sells fudge, cakes, and cookies., 5. I wore a yellow coat in the rain.

page 63

The first letter in each sentence should be capitalized.

page 64

1. Patty played on the baseball team., 2. Patty hit two home runs., 3. She caught the ball, too., 4. What time is it?, 5. Is it time for lunch?

page 65

1.–5. Each sentence should end with a period., 6. Ms., 7. Mr., 8. Mrs., 9. Dr., 10. Ms.

page 66

1. !, 2. ?, 3. ?, 4. !, 5. don't, 6. I'll, 7. didn't, 8. We'll

page 67

1. were not, weren't, 2. was not, wasn't, 3. has not, hasn't, 4. have not, haven't, 5. did not, didn't, 6. are not, aren't, 7. is not, 8. do not, 9. was not, 10. has not, 11. did not, 12. had not, 13. does not, 14. are not, 15. isn't, 16. don't, 17. didn't

page 68

1. a friend's house, 2. Mike's toy, 3. the farmer's bucket, 4. the car's tires, 5. Val's picture, 6. Judy's bike, 7. the bird's nest, 8. the bakery's bread, 9. Mr. Smith's desk, 10. Ally's pen

page 69

June 8, 2013 / Dear Grandmother, / The tag says it comes from Chicago, Illinois. / Love,

page 70

1. Akron, Ohio, 2. Hilo, Hawaii, 3. Macon, Georgia, 4. Nome, Alaska, 5. Provo, Utah, 6. Nancy lives in Barnet, Vermont., 7. Mr. Hill went to Houston, Texas., 8. Did Bruce like Bend, Oregon?, 9. Will Amy visit Newark, Ohio?

page 71

1. Dec. 12, 1948, 2. Mar. 27, 1965, 3. Sept. 8, 1994, 4. Nov. 1, 2000, 5. Jan. 5, 1995, 6. August 10, 1967, 7. Oct. 17, 1983, 8. February 8, 2013, 9. July 29, 2008, 10. Sept. 3, 2010, 11. Oct. 20, 2012, 12. Answers will vary.

page 72

1. hat, 2. bee, 3. cow, 4. dog

page 73

1. informal, 2. formal, 3. informal, 4. formal, 5. formal

page 74

1. road, 2. home, 3. sad, 4. sick, 5. gift, 6. small, 7. large,
8. dog, 9. yell, 10. great, 11. dad, 12. sleep

page 75

1. soft, 2. long, 3. dark, 4. on, 5. happy, 6. low, 7. dry,
8. slow, 9. bad, 10. cold, 11. go, 12. hard

page 76

1. a, 2. b, 3. a, 4. a, 5. a, 6. b, 7. a, 8. b, 9. a, 10. a, 11. b,
12. a

page 77

1. hear, 2. here, 3. here, 4. hear, 5. You're, 6. your, 7. you're

page 78

1. write, 2. right, 3. right, 4. write, 5. right, 6. write, 7. right,
8. right, 9. write, 10. right

page 79

1. to, 2. two, 3. to, 4. to, 5. too, 6. two, 7. too, 8. too, 9. to,
10. to, 11. two

page 80

1. their, 2. They're, 3. there, 4. their, 5. there, 6. They're,
7. They're, 8. there, 9. there, 10. Their, 11. there,
12. They're

page 81

1. sunglasses, 2. afternoon, 3. playground, 4. birthday,
5. scrapbook, 6. sunglasses, 7. afternoon, 8. scrapbook

page 82

1. week, 2. help, 3. like, 4. kind, 5. heat, 6. play, 7. add,
8. sad, 9. duck, 10. write

page 83

1. unable; not able, 2. reopened; opened again, 3. unlucky;
not lucky, 4. unfair; not fair, 5. unhappy; not happy,
6. rewind; wind again, 7. rewashed; washed again,
8. uneven; not even, 9. refilled; filled again, 10. reknitted;
knitted again

page 84

1. careful; full of care, 2. harmless; without harm,
3. dreadful; full of dread, 4. hopeful; full of hope,
5. thankful; full of thanks

page 85

Answers will vary. 1. store, shelves; food that you buy,
2. strong winds, swirled, tossed cars; a strong swirling
storm, 3. raced, passed the other runners; quickly, 4. tall
grasses, wide open spaces; a flat grassy place, 5. her beak,
flew away; a kind of bird

page 86

1. crisp, 2. yanked, 3. string, 4. rope, 5. rushed, 6. soft,
7. wind, 8. thrilled, 9. leaped

page 87

Answers will vary.

page 88

Answers will vary. Sentences should be about school safety.

page 89

1. Uncle Joe is a funny man., 2. Dad told us a funny story
about his dog., 3. Firefighters are brave people.

page 90

The first sentence in each paragraph should be circled. The
other sentences should be underlined.

page 91

Top: 3, 2, 4, 1; Bottom: 2, 3, 4, 1

page 92

1. The story takes place at the zoo., 2. They watch the
playful monkeys., 3. They feed the seals.

page 93

Answers will vary.

page 94

Answers will vary.

page 95

1. birds in the writer's backyard, 2. red, tiny, buzz, chirp,
sweetly, 3. Sentences will vary. Be sure that the sentence
supports the topic.

page 96

Answers will vary.

page 97

1. her grandmother, 2. to thank her grandmother

page 98

Answers will vary. Be sure that each section of the letter
has the appropriate information.

page 99

1. how to make a bird feeder, 2. a pine cone, string, peanut
butter, and birdseed, 3. how the bird feeder will give the
birds a snack

page 100

Order of sentences, by column: 3, 4, 5, 1, 2

page 101

1. Many African American people celebrate a holiday called
Kwanzaa., 2. Answers will vary but should be any sentence
in the paragraph except the first.

page 102

Answers will vary.

page 103

Answers will vary.

page 104

1. The Koala, 2. Anita Best, 3. that it is a good book

page 105

Answers will vary.

page 106

1. that a lizard should be the class pet, 2. Answers will vary. A lizard is small and easy to care for., A lizard is interesting to watch., Students could study the lizard to learn about reptiles., 3. vote for the lizard

page 107

Paragraphs will vary.

page 108

Reports will vary.

page 109

1. 2, 1, 3; air, bat, cat, 2. 3, 2, 1; rock, sea, top, 3. 2, 3, 1; dog, egg, fish, 4. 2, 3, 1; gate, hat, ice, 5. 1, 3, 2; joke, king, lake, 6. 2, 3, 1; mail, neck, owl, 7. 2, 3, 1; walk, yes, zoo, 8. 3, 2, 1; nail, oak, pan

page 110

1. music, noise, poem, 2. plant, rain, sun, 3. frog, garden, ground, 4. afraid, alone, asleep

page 111

1. tiny, 2. no, 3. no, 4. tiny, 5. yes, because the word together falls between tiny and total in ABC order, 6. topic

page 112

1. burst, 2. Grandfather and I burst into laughter., 3. bump, 4. Trash that is left on the ground, 5. Answers will vary.

page 113

1. no, 2. no, 3. yes, 4. no, 5. yes, 6. no, 7. no, 8. no

page 114

1. 8, 2. 4, 3. 10, 4. 3, 5. 11, 6. 4, 7. butterflies, 8. dogs, 9. trees or United States, 10. history, Florida

page 115

1. Kinds of Houses, 2. Jack Builder, 3. 4, 4. page 15, 5. 2, 9

page 116

1. All About Cats, 2. Patricia L. Keller, 3. Richard H. Green, 4. Coaster Press

page 117

1. 5, 2. 1, 3. 7, 4. "Cats in the Wild"

page 118

1. fiction, 2. nonfiction, 3. nonfiction, 4. fiction, 5. fiction, 6. nonfiction, 7. fiction